Munich 1919

The first page of the manuscript of Klemperer's 1942 memoirs on the Revolution of 1918–19.

VICTOR KLEMPERER
Munich 1919

Diary of a Revolution

With a foreword
by Christopher Clark
and
a historical essay
by Wolfram Wette

Translated by Jessica Spengler

polity

First published in German as *Man möchte immer weinen und lachen in einem. Revolutionstagebuch 1919*
© Aufbau Verlag GmbH & Co. KG, Berlin 2015

This English edition © Polity Press, 2022

The translation of this work was supported by a grant from the Goethe-Institut which is funded by the German Ministry of Foreign Affairs.

Polity Press
65 Bridge Street
Cambridge CB2 1UR, UK

Polity Press
350 Main Street
Malden, MA 02148, USA

ISBN-13: 978-1-5095-1059-7 (pb)

A catalogue record for this book is available from the British Library.

Library of Congress Cataloging-in-Publication Data

Names: Klemperer, Victor, 1881-1960, author.
Title: Munich 1919 : diary of a revolution / Victor Klemperer.
Other titles: Man mochte immer weinen und lachen in einem. English
Description: English edition. | Cambridge, UK ; Malden, MA : Polity, 2017. |
    First published in German as Man mochte immer weinen und lachen in einem
    : Revolutionstagebuch 1919. | Includes bibliographical references and
    index.
Identifiers: LCCN 2016048318 (print) | LCCN 2016055458 (ebook) | ISBN
    9781509510580 (hardback) | ISBN 9781509510610 (Mobi) | ISBN 9781509510627
    (Epub)
Subjects: LCSH: Klemperer, Victor, 1881-1960--Diaries. | Bavaria
    (Germany)--History--Revolution, 1918-1919--Sources. | Munich
    (Germany)--History--20th century--Sources. | Young
    men--Germany--Munich--Diaries. | Philologists--Germany--Munich--Diaries. |
    Jews--Germany--Munich--Diaries.
Classification: LCC PC2064.K5 A3 2017 (print) | LCC PC2064.K5 (ebook) | DDC
    943.085092 [B] --dc23
LC record available at https://lccn.loc.gov/2016048318

Typeset in 11/15 Adobe Garamond by
Servis Filmsetting Ltd, Stockport, Cheshire
Printed in the USA by Edwards Brothers

For further information on Polity, visit our website: politybooks.com

Contents

Foreword

Christopher Clark

The wave of political tumult and revolution that crashed over Germany at the end of World War I was a key episode in twentieth-century history. A society already scarred by war and defeat found itself once again shaken to its very foundations. The emergence of a Soviet-style communist Left on the one hand and heavily armed, counter-revolutionary right-wing radical groups on the other led to drastic political polarization. The rhetorical escalation soon degenerated into violence. Freikorps troops clashed fiercely with Spartacists.

Nowhere was the expansion of the conventional political spectrum more dramatic than in Munich. On November 7, 1918, the King of Bavaria became the first German monarch to be toppled. The army defected to the revolutionaries and the king went into exile. After the Bavarian prime minister Kurt Eisner (Independent Social Democratic Party) was assassinated on February 21, 1919, the power struggle between left-wing and moderate socialists came to a head. The government of the new prime minister, Johannes Hoffmann (Social Democratic Party), was overthrown on April 7 and replaced with a Bavarian council republic led initially by pacifist and anarchist intellectuals. But barely a week later, the communists under Eugen Leviné seized power. Hoffmann's cabinet, which had gone into exile, now asked the government in Berlin for help. In mid-April, Reichswehr troops and Freikorps units advanced on the Bavarian revolutionaries. The council republic was then brutally crushed, and an estimated 2,000 of its supporters – both actual and merely alleged – were murdered, summarily shot or sentenced to imprisonment.

Victor Klemperer guides us through the turmoil of these eventful Munich days with empathy, sensitivity, and a perceptive eye. This volume brings together contemporary accounts written for the *Leipziger Neueste Nachrichten* newspaper, only a fraction of which were published at the time, as well as related passages from a later memoir that Klemperer was forced to abandon in 1942. Thanks to the diaries he kept during the Third Reich, Victor Klemperer is one of the most frequently read eyewitnesses of the twentieth century. The keen judgment, eye for striking details, and literary talent he displays in that epic chronicle are also evident in the writings of the young Romance philologist in Munich who was concerned about his academic future.

This is Klemperer describing the entrance of the troops that crushed the council republic in the Bavarian capital in early May 1919:

> . . . all through the day and late into the afternoon, as I write these lines, a thunderous battle has raged. An entire squadron of planes is crisscrossing Munich, directing fire, drawing fire itself, dropping flares; bombs and grenades blast constantly, sometimes farther away, sometimes nearer, shaking the houses, and a torrent of machine-gun fire follows the explosions, with infantry fire rattling in between. And all the while new troops march, drive, ride down Ludwigstrasse with mortars, artillery, forage wagons and field kitchens, sometimes accompanied by music, and a medical train has stopped at the Siegestor, and heavy patrols and various weapons divisions are scattering through the streets, and crowds of people form on every corner that provides cover but also a view, often with opera glasses in their hands.

The reader's attention is drawn dynamically from the airplanes above to the masses of troops below; our gaze sweeps over the multitude of weapons, people, and vehicles, coming to rest on the clusters of bystanders taking in the spectacle through opera glasses. Klemperer memorably conveys the theatricality of the political events, the element of drama about them. In fact, he considers this a defining characteristic of the Munich revolution: "In other revolutions, in other times, in other places," he writes in early February 1919, "the leaders have come from the streets, from the factories, from the typing pools of editorial and law offices. In Munich, many of them have come from the bohemian world." Under these circumstances, politics appears to be not a profession but rather a stage upon which dreams (and night-mares) are played out. "I'm a visionary, a dreamer, a poet!" the prime minister Kurt Eisner cries out to a large assembly in the Hotel Trefler. Klemperer looks on in astonishment as Eisner – a "delicate, tiny, frail, stooped little man" in his eyes – elicits clamorous applause from the Munich audience, and he infers that the people of Munich are less interested in politics than in entertainment.

This book is unique in that it superimposes two time periods: the contemporary reports from Munich are supplemented with retrospective passages from Klemperer's memoirs. Klemperer's experiences in Munich are thus placed in their biographical and historical context. The result is a much deeper reflection on the time; aspects of the Munich revolution that sometimes seem absurd to the young man living through them in the spring of 1919 are later viewed in a more tragic light by the persecuted Jew in Nazi Dresden. Looking back, Klemperer recognizes the growing virulence of the burgeoning anti-Semitism in postwar Germany. "I do not want to exaggerate: there were a good many lecturers and students in Munich at the time who very much condemned this eruption of hostility toward Jews, and during my entire time in Munich I was never personally subjected to anti-Semitism, but I did feel depressed and isolated by it." This book is essential reading.

Christopher Clark
May 2015

Notes on the text

1919, writing as "Antibavaricus"
The two-column reports were written by Victor Klemperer in Munich as the revolution was taking place, between February 1919 and January 1920, under the pseudonym of "A.B. correspondent" (= Antibavaricus) for the Leipzig newspaper *Leipziger Neueste Nachrichten*. The majority of these articles are published here for the first time. The newspaper was only able to print one out of three dispatches; in the tumult of the revolution, the others either arrived too late or never reached their destination at all.

1942, looking back on the revolution
The texts set normally were written in 1942 as part of Klemperer's memoirs. They were not included in the collection *Curriculum vitae: Erinnerungen 1881–1918* (1989) because they were originally intended to be part of a longer chapter called "*Privatdozent*" ("Lecturer"), one which remained unfinished after Klemperer was abruptly forced to stop writing in 1942 – when the danger that the Gestapo might discover the manuscript had grown too great. These texts have never been published before.

Politics and the Bohemian World

(From our A.B. correspondent)

Munich, in early February [1919]
The Munich puzzle. – The ur-Bavarians Eisner, Mühsam, and Levien. – The political bohemians. – The communist estate with two kinds of love. – The effect abroad. – Eisner's future prospects.

Munich politics have gone the way of Munich art – you find yourself asking: where are the Munich natives, or the Bavarians? In the arts you would come across names from East Prussia, from Württemberg, names from everywhere – but it was still "Munich" art. And in politics today? It is really not necessary to insinuate that the prime minister is a Galician and cast doubt on his German name.[1] He is by his own admission a Prussian, and a Berliner to boot. And his main opponents on the Left, who are as highly esteemed in some circles as *Eisner*[2] himself – and he is esteemed, even today, though the elections[3] have gone somewhat against him! – even his radical opponents are no more Bavarian than he is. *Erich Mühsam,*[4] the noble anarchist, whose star ascended in the Café des Westens in Berlin and long radiated a soft literary glow in Munich (despite so many noble anarchist lights) before taking on a truly bloody political flush – Mühsam, who by nature was always a benign, helpful, unmartial creature, and whose revolutionary heroism might amuse us even today were it not also perplexing and dangerous, is widely known to have his roots in Berlin's west side[5] – ever since he was transplanted there, that is. He grew up as the son of a Lübeck pharmacist in what was, at the time, a quiet Hanseatic city.

The latest figure to appear is Doctor *Levien*[6] – as reported from Munich, Dr. Levien was recently arrested[7] – who plays the most serious role here in the Workers' and Soldiers' Council[8] and on the Spartacists' side, and who makes the government, which naturally does not want to create any martyrs, more than a little uneasy. To be clear from the outset: Doctor Levien is not a Russian Jew – he has Germanic blood in his veins, he shakes a mane of blond with every vigorous gesture, his eyes flash blue, and his left hand tugs the button nearest his heart on his field-grey uniform when, with his right hand thrust up or out, he refutes the objection that he is a foreigner who should have no say in matters. At least, this is how he appeared and sounded to me at an assembly where he thundered against the "reactionary" Eisner. Admittedly, when he then cast the poor, hereticized Bolshevists in the right light (namely, the gentle, rosy light of human benefaction) and suddenly faced the accusation that he seemed to be exceedingly familiar with Russian affairs, he thundered with the same conviction and emphatic gesticulation as before – only this time, instead of "I served on the battlefield as German!" it was "I was born in Russia!" So there is something slightly amiss with the Bavarianness of this leader of the people, too. No, he was born the son of a German in Russia, he first breathed Russian air, and he was soon to breathe Russian prison air. He was caught up in the Russian revolutionary movement at a tender age, he formed close ties with a Russian revolutionary in prison and later went to Zurich with her. The two studied and lived entirely in the peculiar atmosphere of Russian Switzerland – there have always been a Russian and an English Switzerland amidst the more well-known German, French, and Italian parts of the country. Just before the war, it occurred to Dr. Levien that he would have to fulfill his German military service obligation at the last minute if he did not want to lose his German citizenship. A friend described Munich to him in alluring terms, so he joined the "Lifers"[9] here — and then the war broke out. For a little while he really did serve on the battlefield, and he was even slightly wounded, but he then spent a long time with the rear echelon in the East and at home. It's said that he was brought back here because he was too closely connected to the Bolshevists in the East. And now he is Munich's most radical popular leader.

The Munich puzzle: The Bavarian is so proud of his heritage, so averse to all things foreign, and particularly all things Nordic, which he likes to refer to collectively as "Prussian." Yet who rules now, each in his own circle, but Messrs. Eisner, Mühsam and Levien! A very simple solution to this puzzle has been proposed. They've said of Eisner (and it's all the more true of Levien) that he prevails in Munich because he feuds so fiercely with Berlin. There is certainly something to this. Eisner has — several times, in any case — appealed strongly to Bavarian particularism; and when Levien rages against the bloodhounds Ebert[10] and Scheidemann,[11] who have now been joined by the chief bloodhound Noske,[12] he rages against murderous Berliners and bloodthirsty Prussians. Nonetheless, both men are so entirely un-Bavarian in their character and, above all, in their dialect — something tremendously important here — that anti-Prussianism alone cannot explain the possibility of their leadership.

No, Munich politics are like Munich art: you need not be either a native Bavarian or a native of Munich to participate. And this is not just a comparison — in Munich, art and politics are the same thing! This, then, is the solution to the puzzle. In other revolutions, in other times, in other places, the leaders have come from the streets, from the factories, from the typing pools of editorial and law offices. In Munich, many of them have come from the bohemian world. We just have to take into consideration — and here's a job for future cultural historians and novelists — that the concept of bohemianism, its ambit, expanded during the war. Before 1914, bohemians were poets or painters or journalists or musicians. And even today they are all of these things, either by profession or avocation. But now they have also become politicians, economists – to put it more simply and clearly: they're also very interested in contraband and profiteering, they've taken an interest (mostly negative) in the relationship between the individual and the masses, they've generally turned their attention, as it were, to the things outside the arts and culture section of the newspaper that they had previously scorned as being unaesthetic. The connection between the bohemian world and politics is as close as can be here in Munich. Is Eisner not thoroughly bohemian, does he not consider himself an artist and writer, as he himself repeatedly insists? But the people of Munich do not demand that their bohemians be Bavarian; perhaps they think true Munich blood is too good for this crowd. *The bohemians of Munich are a foreign legion*, kept for the amusement, the fun of the citizens of Munich. And now artistic amusement has been replaced by political fun . . .

This all sounds very comical and very exaggerated. But anyone who gives it serious thought will find it's not such an exaggeration after all, that I have merely highlighted, isolated, divested of all incidentals, laid bare and thus – to speak in the inviting aesthetic manner – stylized one central aspect of the local political scene. And as far as comedy is concerned, there's certainly an overabundance. In one of these expanded bohemian circles, from which a well-trodden path leads straight to Eisner's office, an amiable, fresh-faced blond lad recently told me, "We're communists, we bought an estate near Augsburg in order to farm it and prove that we can lead an idyllic life in a new community, peacefully, without money." I asked whether one could join by contributing to the investment costs – by buying one's way in, so to speak, as in a cooperative. No, it couldn't be done with money. "So how did you do it?" – "We borrowed it, we don't actually own anything ourselves, we've been good friends for a long time, and if someone has a benefactor he helps out the others." – "Are there farmers in your group?" – "One woman is a gardener; the rest are students, merchants and what the bourgeoisie calls the 'derailed.'" – "So there are women in your community, too?" – "Two so far." – "What's your communism's position on women?" – "We reject legitimate marriage as paid prostitution. Other than that, there are two schools of thought which are still fighting it out. One wants couples to cohabit freely, along the lines of old common-law marriage. The other wants to overcome sexuality entirely; it won't be important anymore." – "How so?" – "We all live in friendly, unsexual fellowship; if the beast stirs in two people, they simply feed the beast and everything goes back to how it was. It's inconsequential, inessential, a triumph over the carnal. That's what we progressives think. But as I said, opinions still differ on this." – "And where do the two ladies in your community stand?" – "The gardener belongs to the older school of thought, the student to the new one". . .

Granted, this is very comical and it's just one example of many. But there is a deadly serious side to this intertwining of bohemianism and politics. For instance, an Italian journalist, a reporter for a large newspaper, traveled from Innsbruck to Munich and now wanders around here freely in order to report on German attitudes and circumstances. He doesn't understand German, but some people in the bohemian circles here understand Italian. The man has acquired a helpful guide from this circle, and it is in this circle that he gathers his impressions, which he faithfully reports back to Turin. I was there when an enthusiastic Spartacus man explained the German situation to him at the tea table: We must and will bring about the dictatorship of the proletariat. It just requires a little educational work. Then all of the imbecile tradesmen, farmers, doctors, academics – in brief, everyone who currently calls themselves bourgeois – will realize with astonishment and delight that they are not bourgeois at all, they are actually proletarians themselves, so they are destined to partake in the unjustly feared and ill-reputed dictatorship of the proletariat. We have at most 100,000 members of the middle class, bourgeoisie and capitalists in Germany. They bought off some of the herd that elected the reactionary National Assembly and kept the rest in stupidity and ignorance. The dictatorship is directed only against these 100,000, and if a little more blood should flow – well, a few drops more or less makes no difference. We have to follow through to pure socialism, like the exemplary Bolshevists who have simply been smeared by the lying press . . . All of this over tea, all of it in very passable Italian, all of it directed at readers abroad . . .

Incidentally, it is this more radical section of the political bohemian world that *Kurt Eisner* will have to thank if – and this is a very real possibility – he should remain at the helm after the state assembly[13] has convened, although the distribution of votes is not to his advantage. He has already shifted somewhat to the right in order not to ruin his chance of continuing to govern from the outset. He also faces fierce enough opposition from the Spartacist quarter. But despite all the hostility, he gets along with these radicals because they are united by their background, their former circle – their bohemianism. So some kind of peace can probably be maintained if Eisner, even a more moderate Eisner, remains in power – but there could never be a moment of peace between any of the bourgeoisie and Munich's bohemian radicals. If Eisner stays, he can thank Levien and Mühsam for it. Their opposition has pushed him closer to the bourgeoisie. At the same time, the bourgeoisie views Eisner as a shield between them and the group around Levien and Mühsam, who feud with him but do not seriously attack him. They feel too much affinity with him for that. They are hostile brothers, but they are brothers all the same – in bohemianism.

Revolution

I slept undisturbed until the early morning, when we reached the German border.[14] From that point on I had changing and diverse company throughout the day: civilians, soldiers from different units, sailors. Everyone talked about the revolution, of course, and I was able to gather from all the stories that it hadn't gone as peacefully everywhere as it had in Leipzig and Wilna; most people also thought that the real trouble still lay ahead of us, that there was no way the Spartacus group would give up without a fight. Two sailors were certain something would happen the next day in Berlin. I told them I intended to spend the night there, in part to visit my relatives,[15] in part to avoid waking my wife.[16] "You'd be better off traveling straight through," they said. "Who knows if you'll be able to get a train tomorrow?" So I switched directly from the Friedrichstrasse to the Anhalter station; a chatty old porter carted my luggage to the tram on Dorotheenstrasse and pointed out houses where shots had been fired. "I had a cartload, and suddenly a machine gun goes off. So I duck into a hallway, and shots start coming from the other side, too, and people crawl in from the tram – it was a real scramble. Afterwards they hauled out three officers and a few of the youth militia and put 'em right up against the wall and threw 'em in the Spree."

I had assumed that after stopping over very briefly I would travel on from Leipzig and report to the Munich regiment.[17] But on this inform-ative journey, I also learned that one could no longer assume a soldier would to try to reach his specified destination; once you had slipped the grasp of your company or battery you could go anywhere, and as long as you didn't make any demands for pay or plunder, you could consider yourself discharged – because which authority would really want to fish around for a single person in the general chaos? Neither of us wanted to go to Munich, and we would arrive early enough for the start of the semester; and besides, I liked to have my military papers in order, so I decided to try to arrange my discharge from Leipzig. I would say that important family and professional matters tied me to Leipzig for a time. But it initially appeared as if this wouldn't work. At the railway station command post and at headquarters, which I visited one after the other, I found the same situation: clusters of men in field-gray uniforms crowded around the desks of common soldiers with red armbands. The soldiers scribbled relentlessly, and every now and then, without looking up or putting down their pens, they would refuse and rant, rant and refuse. The surrounding clusters of men ranted right back, of course – it was an ongoing spectacle. "All they're doing," one of the rejected men told me, "is writing out tickets to the reserve unit and refusing home leave. They're sworn to this yes-and-no and you can't get anything else out of them. No exceptions." Resigned, I left. On the stairs I encountered a private, an older man with the look of an intellectual. He must have held some office in the revolutionary administration because he, too, wore the red armband. "Comrade," I said, "nothing can be done in there, they're just following procedure – can you help me?" And I briefly explained what I wanted. "You can do that," he replied. "Write it up as a petition to the Bavarian Ministry of War and bring it to me this afternoon in the information office at the railway station – Private Hermann." Once there, he wrote "Promptest attention requested by the Leipzig Workers' and Soldiers' Council" at the bottom of my page, stamped the petition and envelope, stamped my ticket as well and issued ration coupons to me on it "until further notice."

Now I could spend a few weeks living in the old way, in my old social circle[18] – but even better than before! The war was at an end, I was really free to do my work, and it had a sure objective, because even though I pinned little hope for the future on my Munich lectureship,[19] at least it definitely belonged to me and couldn't slip through my hands like the professorship in Ghent.[20] And the revolution wouldn't bother me. I wanted to work, just work, return to *L'Astrée*,[21] prepare a large course of lectures on literary history. On the whole I managed to do this, but the revolution could not really be shut out; it was always there, from morning to evening. In the morning, my barber told me how many rifles he had bought, ten marks apiece, from soldiers who were disarming on their own initiative, and how he could easily unload the weapons for twice the price. In the evening, I went to a lecture at the Modern Languages Society. Becker,[22] still very friendly, had personally invited me. I wore my uniform; there was no obligation to salute and no curfew anymore, and civilian clothing had to be spared. On the stairs an agitated student approached me, wanting to know whether I was part of the Soldiers' Council, whether I had come to confirm that the event was innocuous. The lecture had been prohibited an hour previously, access to the building had been blocked by the military, and the erroneous order had only been lifted twenty minutes earlier after entreaties by telephone. The Soldiers' Council had sensed a counter-revolutionary gathering was in the works, as there had recently been a quarrel about hoisting the red flag over the university and the rector had stepped down. Afterwards, Becker – speaking in French, which flowed more smoothly from his lips than German – gave an entirely unpolitical commentary on three symbolic poems by Victor Hugo in front of a handful of students and teachers. Incidentally, this was the first time I heard about the academic situation in Dresden, with which I was completely unfamiliar. For his lecture, Becker handed out a sheet with the three Hugo poems as if they were the lyrics of a concert program. The pages had originally been printed for a summer course in Dresden which had been thwarted by the war. There was a technical college there with all sorts of literary and philosophical ambitions, even with a proper chair of Romance philology. The occupant of this chair, Heiss,[23] had been sent to Dorpat in some administrative capacity during the war, and Becker had stood in for him in Dresden. These fleeting reminders of the revolution, such as the barber dealing in arms or the fear of sedition in the Modern Languages Society, cropped up day in and day out, and I learned from the newspapers and my conversations with Harms[24] and Kopke[25] that tensions were growing all over Germany, and that people everywhere, Leipzig included, were expecting civil war to erupt at any moment. But Harms and Kopke viewed the situation very coolly, as if with purely professional interest, and Hans Scherner,[26] who had always been apolitical, was entirely absorbed in his studies for his matriculation exam,[27] and my wife spent every remaining hour that was granted to her in Leipzig thinking fervently about her organ studies.[28] So I, too, pushed away all emotions and distractions and focused all the more intently on preparing for my teaching position, since people were now starting to talk about special courses for students returning home from the war. Only once did I attend a political gathering; I wanted to get to know the most radical of them all. The Spartacus people met in the Coburger Hallen, a rather dismal tavern on the Brühl. Judging from the pictures on the wall, the long, smoky room had been the meeting place for a railroad workers' association; above the many group photos of engineers and conductors hung a large portrait of Kaiser Wilhelm[29] with his cuirassier helmet and his Haby mustache.[30] About 250 people sat tightly packed at two long tables, smoking and drinking beer, most of them men of various ages, the majority probably workers. The scene was so utterly peaceful that it could well have been a regular meeting of railroad workers, or a presentation by a rabbit breeders' club or group of amateur gardeners. Even the speaker's matter-of-fact tone fitted with this supposition, as long as you listened only to the sound of his slow, deliberately formed sentences. Their content therefore affected me all the more. The speaker, a hulking soldier of about forty, East Prussian judging by his accent, proved to his silent audience the necessity of civil war, just as a schoolteacher would develop a mathematical theorem. "We are the poor," he said, "and the uneducated. The revolution has not helped us at all, a bourgeois republic has been created, the government socialists have betrayed us – they are at least as hostile toward us as the other parties on the Right. The press belongs to the propertied and educated classes; under the universal freedom of the press, we alone are not free. The propertied and educated classes will make up the majority of the planned National Assembly;[31] we will be in the minority and have just as little influence there as we now have in the press. There is no universal freedom that can help us, at least not for the time being. We must prevent the formation of the National Assembly, we must take the press entirely into our hands and only our hands, we must establish and maintain the dictatorship of the proletariat until all property has been socialized and until we get the education we have been denied. This can only be achieved by force. And why shouldn't we use force? So much blood has been spilled for the capitalist cause, why shouldn't a little flow for the proletarian cause as well?" The audience nodded, shouted bravo, applauded, all very seriously, with conviction, and without over-exuberance. A second speaker, this time a civilian, undoubtedly a local master craftsman, began to paraphrase the remarks of the East Prussian. "Abominable waste of time," I thought, and I left. I did not sympathize in the least with these people. I hoped that the government would succeed in keeping them in check without bloodshed. But if it were not possible without violence, well, then hopefully the government was strong enough to assert itself and follow through on the election of the National Assembly. What the Spartacist had decried as bourgeois freedom was, to me, the epitome of all that was politically good, and it had to meet the needs of everyone, even the proletarian worker – and freedom could only spread to an entire people if it came from the center. Perhaps the revolution had come at an unfortunate time, but I wholeheartedly approved of the new government's principles (just as I still love the Weimar Constitution to this day).[32] If I did have any sympathy for the opponents of the republic, it was only with respect to the opposition on the Right. We had to endure such terrible things from our adversaries; perhaps without the revolution we would not have been quite so defenseless against them after all. Could it possibly have been avoided without an internal collapse? "In Aachen (or in

Jülich)," I noted, "a Belgian commander decreed that German civilians must honor the officers of the occupation by stepping from the sidewalk and doffing their hats, under penalty of summary execution. Granted, this summer Beyerlein[33] told me we did the exact same thing in Romania, and today Kopke said, 'In Poland, too' – but it makes me quite miserable to think of this humiliation." But if I sympathized a tiny bit with the opposition on the Right, it was in the belief that they posed no threat to the new system of government. I thought that they would form the right wing of the National Assembly, not try to demolish the republic. But it was not hard for me to push all of these thoughts aside and devote myself entirely to pre-Classical and Classical French literature. For all of the editorials and assemblies, Leipzig was deeply serene, and in Café Merkur the rustle of newspapers mixed with the slap of skat cards. Of course, my devotion did not entirely cut me off from the present. "The cruelties of the French!" I wrote in another diary entry from the time. "How is it possible that one and the same people can behave in such a cruelly vindictive and ignoble way and yet produce such gloriously humane literature?" This was the question that would shape the development of my program of literary history and *Kulturkunde*[34] (the word was still unfamiliar to me, and to this day I do not know when it was first used, or by whom) in the coming years.

In mid-December I traveled to Munich – alone, and hoping to stay for just a few days. I had four items on my agenda, but a fifth, unforeseen one subsequently proved to be the most significant. On the journey there I first experienced what would become my principal memory of all trips taken during the revolutionary period: I couldn't find a way onto the overcrowded train through the regular door or completely blocked corridors, but there were always some fellows standing around in uniform or civilian dress who would hoist me up to a window or bundle me out of one. The first time this happened, on the evening of December 10th in Leipzig, was the snappiest and most in keeping with the style of the revolution: two sailors hauled me aboard with a loud "heave-ho!" and a single jerk. Of the many different scenes that played out on the long, frequently delayed journey, two stayed with me. An old Saxon reservist ruefully contended that Germany was suffering the misery of the revolution on account of its sins. He was laughingly contradicted by a cocky lad from Hamburg, the most vivid caricature of a revolutionary I had ever seen. His unruly blond mane tumbled into bold blue eyes, and his neck bore a gaping red scar that could just as easily have been acquired in a dockside brawl at home as on the front line. A red band was tied around the arm of his uniform jacket, and across his chest he wore a sash more than a hand's breadth wide, the ends of which hung down over his belt. The boy said the revolution was a joy and a salvation. He himself was taking a study trip through Germany to see where it was proceeding most efficiently. He boasted of getting a free ride wherever he went, as there was always a soldiers' council willing to give him train tickets, accommodation and food. The other scene, which unfolded on the Bavarian side of the border the next morning, seemed to have come straight from a pre-naturalist comedy. A white-haired Swabian uncle had picked up his two nieces from boarding school and was taking them home. He wanted to protect the innocents, but he also had to guard the luggage stowed in the lavatory. In his absence, the high-spirited girls took the opportunity to befriend some jocular soldiers, who gave them cigarettes and a light. The girls laughed, smoked and coughed, the soldiers teased, the old man pleaded and scolded, then disappeared mid-sentence because he feared for the luggage, then returned, agitated, to implore and rebuke them some more. Munich, which I reached at noon the next day, three hours late, presented the most surprising scene of all. How often had I compared Leipzig's teeming life with Munich's parochial drowsiness in my diary in recent years. But now! If I might be forgiven a paradox, I would write that now things were entirely the other way around: Leipzig was in a state of the soberest tranquility, while Munich at first glance was a vision of the extraordinary, the colorfully and passionately romantic. The city was richly decked with multicolored flags. Bavarian blue and white prevailed, but black and yellow (Munich's city colors) and the black, red, and gold of Greater Germany and the republic were not uncommon and roughly balanced each other out; revolutionary red was scarce, but it fluttered from significant buildings such as the Residence and the Ministry of War. It was not clear to me whether this abundance of flags (which was missing only the old imperial black, white, and red) was for the benefit of the regiments returning home from the front or a sign of continuing joy at the rapid victory of the revolution. The homecoming troops were brought to mind by two obelisks entwined with fir garlands and inscribed "1914–1918" in front of the Field Marshals' Hall, the revolution by the many newspaper stands and pamphlet sellers, along with posters on the walls and bills on the advertising pillars. Where military dispatches had once hung, a public notice had now been pasted warning that firearms would be used "without leniency" against anyone disturbing the peace "from the Right or Left," and on the pillars, giant posters were squeezed between the advertisements with an appeal to the population, in view of the fuel shortage, to bring an end to "wild jaunts with ladies in army vehicles." But what was remarkable was not the wealth of newspapers, flyers, and posters; it was that all of this literature attracted a lively audience. Clusters of people formed around every pillar and wall and newspaper stand, even around criers in the middle of the pavement, the people in the center debating, the ones on the edges craning in. In the months that followed, these clusters of people would become a familiar and reliable signal for me. They always reminded me of the bubbles that form in milk just a few seconds before it boils over: as soon as the little round clusters appeared, I knew that within twenty-four hours at the latest there would definitely be a streetcar strike, almost certainly a general strike, and very probably a firefight. But back in December this phenomenon was entirely new to me, and at the time it still lacked any toxic virulence – that did not change until Eisner was murdered.[35] The people seemed merely innocuously excited and amused; it was a bit of fun, a political carnival. The amusement of the public was particularly apparent among the many soldiers, who were worlds apart from their Saxon comrades. They wore their round field caps at a rakish angle, they wore red and blue decorations in the form of bows, ribbons, and little flowers on their shoulders and chests, they bore reservists' batons with long ribbons of every color. (Black, white, and red was the only combination they avoided, just as the imperial cockade was missing from their caps, leaving only the Bavarian one.) The jolliest scenes were found wherever a long line of common soldiers stood waiting at a bootblack's stand. Oh, how the *Schniggel*[36] fretted about shiny boots! I think he felt the triumph of the revolution and his hard-won freedom most intensely when he placed his foot on the shoe-shine step and let someone else serve him. There is a lovely verse in one of Paul Heyse's poems from Italy, "Boot Sonnet," where he describes the grand air with which a poor devil has his shoes cleaned on the street. The poem ends with something like: "If you have a *soldo*, you can get them shined, and if you get them shined, you are a *signore*."[37] I so often criticized the false *Italianità* of the Field Marshals' Hall and Ludwigstrasse, the beer bellies and beer hearts of Munich's petite bourgeoisie. I think I did them a slight injustice; I think there is an Italian aspect about them after all, one which lies dormant under a cushion of fat for years before suddenly bursting forth in all of its animal childishness, sometimes good, sometimes bad, sometimes comic, sometimes tragic. Yet another thing distinguished the cityscape of Munich from that of Leipzig and amplified the carnivalesque atmosphere. In Leipzig, the only foreign soldiers one encountered were the occasional band of Russian prisoners looking miserable and humble and quite inconspicuous. In Munich, dapper French soldiers sauntered through the streets. They were fine fellows in fine uniforms, officers, staff sergeants, chaps from commissions of some kind, their red trousers blazed, their gray-blue uniform jackets and overcoats were impeccably tailored, and the soft, dark velvet caps of the alpine rangers looked more dashing and less proletarian than the cocked hats of the Bavarian infantrymen. These people clearly radiated victory, but they seemed neither vindictive nor haughty, merely cheerful and pleased with their reception. And evidently for good reason, as they drew no hostile looks but some approving ones, and not only from women. I think the war no longer existed for the Bavarians. The war had been the business of the Prussianized empire, after all; the empire was over,

Bavaria was itself once again, and why shouldn't the freshly baked Free State maintain comradely relations with the French Republic? Just because of a past scuffle? A scuffle needn't come between comrades.

But all of these thoughts only came to me later. For the time being all I noticed were the streetscapes. My mind was occupied with the four items I hoped to attend to as swiftly as possible. The list on the slip of paper in my vest pocket read: (1) university, (2) Ministry of War, (3) housing, (4) Kraftmair. Item 4 was dealt with most quickly and easily. Kellermann, the archetype of Wolzogen's "Kraftmayer,"[38] whom I knew only as a pipe-smoking raconteur from his vacations in Urfeld, was a professor at the music academy in Munich, and I was supposed to ask him whether and how my wife could continue her organ studies here. He was very friendly toward me. He said he would do what he could to ensure that my wife – who had studied at a conservatory and frequently given concerts as a pianist in years past – would be spared the usual admission formalities and mandatory secondary subjects so that she could dedicate herself immediately and entirely to her own affairs. A few practice organs would be available, too. (Kellermann was, admittedly, all too optimistic on this point, and my wife's complaints did not cease until she was able to take refuge in the Protestant church on the Stachus square. There she sat and played while gunfire rattled outside and bullets caused plaster to rain down from the walls of the church.) The housing issue was dealt with nearly as swiftly, though not nearly as successfully. In a single hour I was done with the three main property offices: the municipal housing authority, the Homeowners' Bank, and Lion real estate. All of them together had only three three-room apartments to offer, the cheapest of which would have cost 2,000 marks a year. Larger apartments were almost as scarce and correspondingly more expensive. But for us, even 2,000 marks was prohibitive. "Perhaps," said the young woman at the municipal housing authority, "you could rent a studio with adjoining rooms." – "Very well," I said, "can you suggest one?" – "We can't, but try the Homeowners' Bank or Lion." The Homeowners' Bank said "try Lion," and Lion said they had "just rented the last studio yesterday." Our furniture had been in storage with Wetsch[39] since the winter of 1915. It would stay there until the end of 1920. The housing shortage was growing everywhere. I visited the housing authority in Dresden so often that the friendly secretary finally said, despairingly, "I dreamed about you last night, Professor." – My military and academic affairs took somewhat more time. They came to a satisfactory conclusion, but each situation was also *"underleinet,"*[40] to quote Walther von der Vogelweide, with a certain bitterness. The Bavarian Ministry of War had not responded to my petition for discharge, which had been approved by the Leipzig Soldiers' Council. I went there now, and at the warden's booth I showed my papers from Wilna and the order from Munich[41] to which I owed my escape from Wilna. An orderly then led me to the minister's antechamber, where paintings of battles from another age still hung and there was a good deal of coming and going. After a while a young man in civilian clothing asked if I absolutely had to speak to the minister in person. I thought not. "Then let's take you to the adjutant." The adjutant, also young, wearing a lieutenant's uniform but addressed as "Doctor," knew my name from the university, was very polite and helpful and, after the briefest consideration, dictated to a typist: "Sergeant Klemperer, whose other documents are to be requested from the Wilna Press Office, is hereby transferred to the 7th Bavarian Field Artillery Regiment, Replacement Division, to be discharged. The Minister of War – *per pro.*," illegible signature. I then spent two days wandering extensively around the familiar old Alphons School and Max II barracks.[42] The barracks were flying the blue-and-white flag as well as the red and had recently been decorated with fir boughs in anticipation of the regiment's return. The soldiers had no duties besides decorating, but typewriters clacked in the offices, there was work to be done in the storerooms, and the doctor and medics were busy. An older gentleman in civilian clothing was referred to as the commander and lieutenant colonel, but the actual authority lay with the Soldiers' Council. In the infirmary, where I had to be examined, I saw a scene characteristic of the new circumstances. A heavy country boy stood half naked and crimson-faced before the youthful doctor, every limb

trembling in a real or feigned fit, I couldn't tell which. With easy
humor the doctor said, "I can be just as pigheaded as you. Trembling
and raging won't get you anywhere with me. Pluck up your courage
and ask me proper instead of getting smart with me, then you'll get
your leave. Think it over, my friend." I don't know where his thoughts
got him because I was finished by then. Being discharged in this way
can work out painlessly or painfully, favorably or unfavorably; there are
many regulations, and all of them are elastic, and it all comes down to
the goodwill of many little office dictators. I fared very well. It touched
me to be greeted warmly as a battlefield comrade by people whose
names had escaped me. The clothing store was still under the control of
the fat Sergeant Langermeyer, who had been well disposed toward me
right from the start, back in July of '15. And in an important office I
ran into Zinsmeister, the friendly mechanic from the Plouichferme.[43]
He was a sergeant now and wore the Iron Cross First Class, he looked
radiant, and his uniform was as tidy as if he were five minutes away
from reporting to Major General Hopf for a troop inspection.
Zinsmeister told me about the fate of our sixth battery, which had led
such a peaceful existence during my time at the front. In the course of
the final offensive and then during the fighting retreat, it had repeatedly come under fire and suffered heavy losses. Ruhl, my nemesis and
my doom,[44] had been severely wounded. I ate with Zinsmeister in the
canteen for non-commissioned officers and privates: big baked dump-
lings in a fruit soup, neatly arranged on china plates which still bore the
old PRL[45] regimental insignia in blue. How I had longed, in 1915, to
be delivered from the feed stall and tin cups of the troops to this finer
location and tableware! Now I was an enfranchised comrade here and
practically a celebrated guest. Every conceivable kindness was extended
to me. A good deal of retroactive pay was calculated for me; I received
four weeks of "convalescent leave" prior to my final discharge (for
which the papers from Wilna were needed), which meant additional
pay and tickets to Berlin, Leipzig, and Kipsdorf ("second class, 'cause
you had kidney problems!"); I received woollen underwear and sturdy
new trousers ("you can dye 'em, you won't see the like of that cloth

again!") and brand new boots with laces made of real cord. These were true treasures. I also received ration coupons ("no need to report 'em!") and even a few actual bread rations. My certificate of discharge ("nothin' more you need to do") would be sent to me in January (and it was). And yet there was a bitterness to these hours. I was reminded all too vividly of what I had endured here in 1915, the repetition of which I had so often dreaded. There was the gate of the Alphons School, where I had stood inside and waited for my wife every evening. Many days I wasn't allowed out because I still couldn't salute – me, the volunteer, the thirty-three-year-old, the married man, the university lecturer. There was the ordnance shed where Captain Berghausen had roared in a frenzy that I was to be confined to barracks. There was – but I would have to relive far too much from that chapter of my life as a soldier, because the glut of painful memories from my military time crashed over me then. "All of it," I noted in the evening, "was a bit buried in my memory. The revolution, or at least the revolution at such a fatal moment, garnered little sympathy from me, and now that efforts are being made to establish a true democracy, Spartacus is a thousand times more abhorrent to me than the Right and the officers were in Wilhelm's time. But today, when my bad memories from my time as a soldier suddenly ambushed me (and I do realize that, all in all, very few bad things actually happened to me), today every – and I mean every – absurdity of the revolution made sense to me."

A more lasting and far more significant bitterness attached itself to my academic affairs, which had been the actual reason for my trip. The university intended to make double use of the coming year, so to speak. From February through May an extra "war emergency semester" was to be held with "refresher and continuation courses" for students returning home, and the summer break would be shortened so that two semesters could also be squeezed out of the following autumn and winter. School classes were planned, too, though not for schoolboys with pencil cases. Homecoming soldiers who had gone to war without having finished secondary school were allowed to start studying anything they wanted straight away as long as they took scholastically tinged classes at the university itself in preparation for an informal entrance exam. Vossler[46] had written to say it would be good if I could personally participate in drawing up the Romance "bill of fare" and also heed the call to attend a general faculty meeting. A small group of us quickly put together the program. It fell to me to lecture on French Classicism; I was supposed to teach the returning soldiers not only French but also German, since I had been one of Muncker's students.[47] The faculty meeting that I had looked forward to with such pride was disappointing. I would later come to learn that such "general" or "large" faculty meetings are, without exception, nothing more than mock battles. The decisions are made beforehand by a small coterie of full professors, the discussion of the *gentes minores*[48] is guided, there is not much dissent, and certainly no need to fear a vote because every lecturer eventually wants to become an *extraordinarius*[49] and every *extraordinarius* eventually wants to become an *ordinarius*,[50] and the culture ministries of the individual states hew to the proposals of the faculties (i.e., the full professors), and the faculties of the individual universities are in constant contact with one another. If Lecturer Schulze in Tübingen earns a reputation as a troublemaker, not only will he never rise to the rank of *extraordinarius* in Tübingen, he will also never be considered for an appointment in Erlangen or Rostock either. But in this first faculty meeting I was not yet aware of the powerlessness of the non-professors, because absolutely no decisions were made. We sat in the small auditorium (where I had given my test lecture[51] four years earlier), most of us at a long green table, a few in the window alcoves. These more comfortably seated and sequestered individuals included Vossler, who naturally beckoned Lerch[52] and me over to him, and a stocky man with a head of graying curls and a chubby face as sensuous as it was spirited: the Slavist Berneker.[53] For hours the talk circled quite dully, with repetitions and variations, around just a few questions. Only suppertime hunger seemed to bring an end to the debate, and in closing, Clemens Baeumker,[54] who was presiding in his role as rector, declared the meeting to have been "a gratifying discussion and point of contact with the faculty at a difficult time"! The aim had been to precisely define the "refresher" and "continuation" courses; this was not achieved, and yet it was of very real importance because the refresher courses were to be treated as "tutorials," meaning they would be paid less, while the continuation courses would be remunerated at the full rate for lectures during ordinary semesters. A ministry official had notified an *ordinarius* of the ministry's view on this matter, but his information was neither clear nor binding. An extremely thin, very elegantly dressed, beardless gentleman proposed that the question be ceded to a commission for meritorical discussion. "What's 'meritorical'?"[55] I asked Vossler. "An Austrian word," he said. "What does it mean?" – "Absolutely nothing." – "And who's the speaker?" - "A mind mechanic." This is how he referred to philosophers and psychologists with a scientific bent. Lerch added some personal information: "Kafka,[56] moved here from Vienna to lecture, was a flying officer with the Austrians, his wife is an equestrienne and very modern." (I did not see Kafka again during the rest of my time in Munich, but a few years later he became a colleague of mine in Dresden, and I will have more to say about him.) In the meantime the speeches continued to flow and now revolved almost exclusively around financial issues. Who should pay the lecturer his fees during this war emergency semester: the state or the student? Couldn't the full professors forgo their honorarium for the benefit of the unsalaried lecturers? If the students had to pay lecture fees as in a normal semester, on what basis would a waiver of the full, half or quarter amount be granted? Whenever such a question had been flogged to death, the decision would be made to cede it to a commission for meritorical discussion. A convention of post office clerks or customs officials would doubtless have been on a par with our faculty meeting. And yet I was not bored. Lerch pointed out this and that attendee, so it really was a point of contact for me. The gaunt man with the pinched face who mostly and ostentatiously turned his back on our group was our closest departmental colleague, Jordan,[57] a titular professor at the university and director of the business college, and a bitter enemy of Vossler, whose chair he had wanted for himself. The three near Muncker, as fundamentally different in appearance as they were in disposition and achievement, were his German philology lecturers: the feline-faced Strich,[58] a genteel and already distinguished aesthetician; the tiny squirrel Borcherdt,[59] exceedingly bustling and productive but no better than average, "satisfactory on the whole"; and Janentzky,[60] the giant with the great curly pate (you had to call it a "pate"), a slow, lumbering philosopher, but really a philosophizing literary historian. I shook hands and exchanged a few words with these three afterwards. Then one of the "heavyweight" professors who had been seated next to Baeumker addressed me in a most friendly way, like a close acquaintance, and inquired about my experiences at the front and my plans. He was an old or aged man whom at first I did not recognize at all. His face was rather sunken and pale, but with a bright red nose, he dragged his left foot a little, and his clothing appeared somewhat shabby and ill-kept. Only after he had spoken to me for a good while in a very obliging manner did it dawn on me: this was Crusius,[61] the lofty Hellenist, the faculty bigwig, the audacious war poet of 1914. "Passé," Lerch said. "He hasn't produced anything for ages, he's recently taken up drinking, and he's definitely already had his first very minor stroke." Four weeks later in Café Merkur, I read in the academic obituaries of the *Vossische Zeitung*: "An important researcher and university professor has been wrested from his work by a heart attack at the age of just 60." And a month after that, at her infamous tea party, Martha Muncker[62] recounted with a touch of venom how he had met his happy end: he had returned home in tipsy high spirits and needed some assistance getting to bed, then fell asleep smiling and did not wake up again the next morning. I must say, I much prefer the memory of the friendly potator[63] to that of the pompous humanist.

This faculty meeting was definitely not uplifting, but it certainly gave me no reason to feel dejected in any way. No, the bitterness that tainted the academic part of this trip to Munich came solely from Lerch. It was on this December 13th that he hit upon the topic which, thanks to his endless revisiting of it, would weigh on me for an entire year to the day. Grief over Sonja's death[64] and delight in the suggestive future tense[65] were equally far from his mind now; he mostly seemed filled with social discontent. A lectureship was more of a starveling position than ever, he said, and the hope of a well-salaried professorship more distant than ever. But of all the lecturers, the Romance philologists were the most hopeless, and of all the Romance philologists, no one was in a more futile situation than we two disciples of Vossler, because Vossler's artistic nature and frequent philosophizing made him so objectionable to real philologists. Only the tiniest consolation existed for Lerch under these circumstances: of we two disciples of Vossler, only he, as a grammarian, and because he never stinted on Tobler[66] quotes, had at least a very tiny possibility of acquiring a teaching post at some point; I, on the other hand, as a literary historian – and not even for the Old or Middle French epoch, but for the modern era (because for real philologists, Montesquieu[67] was practically recent literature) – no, honestly, if I couldn't live off my private assets, I would do better to change jobs altogether! – I had no private assets. I thought about my dashed hopes for Posen[68] and Ghent, I thought about Becker's remarks and the unsuccessful ride across Lake Constance,[69] I thought about my agonizing dependency on my brothers,[70] I thought about how prices were rising daily, and I felt quite ill.

These were the four items on the agenda for my trip. The unintended fifth result came about through Hans Meyerhof.[71] He was still leading his harried old beggarly dealer's life in his old smuggler's den, but he had become a different man: he beamed with contentment and an ardor for life. The revolution and the role that had fallen to him in it made him happy. He was an enthusiastic Eisner devotee, and he was convinced that freedom and good fortune would spread from the Bavarian Free State to the rest of Germany and Europe. He knew the prime minister personally, he knew all the leading figures in the new regime personally; they took advice from him, they put him to work for them. During these three December days in Munich, I was somewhat skeptical and thought Hans was pulling my leg a little; I later realized that he really hadn't exaggerated his own importance. From Eisner until the collapse of the Council Republic, he really did play the role of – to put it paradoxically and yet most precisely – an active bystander. I often marveled at his strange idealism. He could easily have been assigned to some lucrative office, even a high one. I saw on multiple occasions that the opportunity was available to him. But he always refused, and always with the same reasoning: "I'm a smuggler, so my hands aren't clean enough to govern." But this refusal was not based on idealistic self-sacrifice alone. Granted, merely standing by did not entirely satisfy Hans, and he was tempted to play the game. But the emphasis here was on "play"; he was too lax and scattered to take on full responsibility, also too soft and, for all of his enthusiasm about the revolutionary cause, too skeptical. So he contented himself with occasionally carrying out small tasks, privately and anonymously and without pay. And this is how peace was maintained between us. I knew that his radicalism would always remain playful and bloodless, and he in turn could count on the fact that I, the "reactionary bourgeois" as he called me, would never put him in danger. We clashed very fiercely a few times in the period that followed, but we were never enemies for more than a night.

As overly busy as my three days in Munich were, Hans did not give in: I had to accompany him to two assemblies. The first time Elena[72] came as well, and because she was hard of hearing we managed to get seats in the front row. The "Political Council of Intellectual Workers" – Hans was a member and had many acquaintances in the audience – around two hundred gentlemen and ladies, by no means merely men and women, all of them clearly intellectuals, academics, artists, bohemians, in an elegant room in the Bayrischer Hof hotel. At the board members' table were half a dozen literary types, at the podium a youngish, clean-shaven man with sparse, receding blond hair, heavy gray-blue eyes, an ample mouth and strong, wide jaw, with a manner and tone suggestive of an officer in civilian clothing, but not a Simplicissimus[73] officer. This was Bruno Frank.[74] At the start of the year I had seen his play *The Sisters and the Stranger*[75] at the Leipzig Playhouse, a heavily Schnitzleresque[76] and yet singular and notable effort. Now he read an essay aloud with good, simple emphasis: "Revolution and Altruism."[77] It was an essay and not a lecture, a literary work and not a political one. It was not rhetorical, and a few times it even strove to address specific issues and economic matters. The bourgeois citizen had to "open his wallet," he had to voluntarily forgo the advantages of property, education, the beautiful life, he had to acknowledge the sovereignty of the people as a whole. All of this was expressed very neatly and warm-heartedly and not all too prettily, it was shot through with fine individual remarks and interesting quotes – including a powerful excerpt from Victor Hugo's oration on Voltaire[78] – but in the end it was merely a pleasing oratorical exercise on a general topic. It was literature. Then the debaters took the podium. One said: "In 1914 you wrote war poems for Germany, and now you're a revolutionary who sympathizes with the Soviets!" Frank responded placidly: "At the time I believed in Germany's innocence" – but the war had changed something inside him. At least a dozen opponents accused him of having generalized and spoken in a purely aesthetic manner. The odd thing was that this same dozen generalized as well. But then a man hurried to the podium, pulling a thick manuscript from his bag as he went. He immediately and abruptly began reading a memorandum on the defects of the university constitution. After two minutes he was interrupted by the chairman and forced to step down. The next speaker was also interrupted multiple times, both from the board members' table and from the audience, but he did not give in and spoke for a quarter of an hour, with practiced pathos but in broken German, about the glory of the Russian councils constitution. He was a brilliant-looking old man with a white mane. "The painter Stückgold,"[79] Hans whispered to me, "official and salaried agent of the Russians." I did not take to the man at all. All the same, he was the only one on this "political council" to talk about something political. A very young man then requested to speak. He said: "The public wants nothing to do with us educated people. I experienced what it was like in public classes as a volunteer teacher, and it was a very bad experience." This was the only time indignation erupted in the room, and gruff words were volleyed about such as "insolent" and "wet behind the ears." I could not shake the thought that they were making such a fuss because he had hit a nerve. Things immediately returned to the peacefully literary, and finally to the comical. A silly blonde with an innocent sweetness about her introduced herself as a librarian at a public reading room and declared that, for her part, she had had the most favorable experiences concerning the people's desire for education. She had captured these delightful and uplifting impressions in a series of poems – and suddenly a notebook was in front of her, and she began relentlessly reciting the most trite and maudlin rhymes. The audience laughed, some shouted "Enough!", others "Freedom of speech!", and still others "But not freedom of poetry!" – but the young woman was undeterred and droned out poem after poem, until finally the entire room clapped so long and so loudly that the applause drowned out everything and forced her to stop. A moment later the chairman announced that the requests to speak had been exhausted, and he ended the "stimulating evening" by thanking the lecturer and all of the speakers. In the end I had laughed as well, but afterward I felt there was something embarrassing and undignified about the whole event.[80] Why was a literary circle pretending to pursue politics, and why were thoroughly bourgeois people flirting with the proletariat by calling themselves a "Political Council of Intellectual Workers"? Hans came to the defense of those I attacked. They felt more affinity with the working proletariat than the capitalist bourgeoisie, he claimed, and even if they were not yet politicians, they had come together precisely for the purpose of their own politicization. I said he should show me his party's proper, mature politicians then. "Tomorrow" – the Independents[81] were holding an election meeting and Eisner himself would speak. The Independent Social Democrats – originally (during the war, that is) a radical wing of the Socialists that had split off under Liebknecht,[82] now in opposition to the government or Majority Socialists in the Reich and in Prussia, but themselves besieged on the Left by the Russian-oriented Spartacus League ("Spartácus" as they said in Munich) – the Independents were Eisner's actual ruling party. This time, at the Trefler[83] on Sonnenstrasse, where carnival balls were held in normal times, I saw not a few hundred well-mannered literati but rather the true people of Munich in their thousands – a vehemently agitated people. When we arrived at around 7, the main entrance had already been closed by the police because of overcrowding, but Hans naturally knew of a side entrance through the utility rooms, and the guard posted there readily believed that he was a "personal friend of the prime minister bearing a personal message." We wound up directly beneath the big dais with the lectern and the board members' table. The giant hall and the galleries running around it were packed full. Rows of chairs were arranged along the wall on the left side of the room, while on the right there were tables with people eating and drinking. A dense crowd thronged between the seats, to the right and left and in the wide central aisle. Waitresses carrying six, eight, or even ten heavy mugs of beer in front of them pushed their way through this seemingly impassable blockade; it was a tremendous feat of strength. People even sat on the edge of the dais, their legs dangling in the room. I thought I recognized a pair of elegant high boots directly under the lectern; someone had once said of a similar pair: "I took them off an officer." Then I saw the ends of a red sash dangling to the accompanying knees and I noticed the wide scar on the neck: my compartment mate from the journey to Munich had arrived here on his study trip through the revolution, and he cut a picturesque figure. A woman at the board members' table opened the meeting and gave the floor to the Minister for Social Affairs, Comrade Unterleitner.[84] He was a brown-haired man in his thirties, and his diction was as Bavarian as his name. He began by shouting in clipped sentences in order to pierce the immense room, but the content of his speech was matter-of-fact. He defended the Independents against the Right and the Left. He warmed up when he talked about the contributions made by women – some of his words were unmistakably in reference to poor Sonja Lerch – and he fell into an astounding and positively religious rapture when he spoke of his prime minister. Some of his sentences stayed with me verbatim, and I noted them down a few hours later. "Kurt Eisner is the sword of the revolution, and not just the Bavarian one, he toppled all twenty-two thrones in Germany. He is our brilliant leader, and I will stand by him forever, and the only way to get to Kurt Eisner is over my dead body."

Even more astonishing than the passion of this individual speaker was the clamorous, minutes-long applause with which each of his declarations of love for Eisner was received. Once again, this was truly a Bavarian people's assembly, quite obviously made up of workers, tradesmen, shopkeepers – and Eisner had been the editor of *Vorwärts* in Berlin, he was "a Prussian and a Jew" (synonyms to many Bavarians). Where had this Munich enthusiasm come from? What kind of man was the prime minister? Then the question of freedom of speech or time limits was debated. The assembly agreed on freedom of speech but did not keep to this agreement. A gentle, hoarse, gaunt man, who represented the cause of the Majority Socialists, was shouted down: "Bourgeois, bourgeois, bourg!" – "I'm a Socialist!" – "You're full of rubbish!" Then piercing whistles and "bourgeois, bourg!" again, until the man disappeared. He was followed by "Doctor Levien from the Spartacus League," blond, blue-eyed, chilly and unabashedly classically handsome. Slender and young, in a well-fitting field-gray uniform with a high collar; a beardless, unlined face; large, commanding eyes, a commanding, penetrating tone; broad, powerful gestures; sweeping pathos – "comrades, companions, citizens" – fierce diatribes against "Ebert and Scheidemann, the bloodhounds in Berlin," revolt against the far too timid and, in truth, reactionary Eisner, a hymn to the unjustly vilified Bolsheviki (impassioned oxytone),[85] swift deflection of all hostile comments – "Were you in Russia?" – "I was born in Moscow." – "You're no Bavarian." – "This is a Bavarian jacket," as he yanks on his uniform with a clenched fist. This man, who immediately made the most distasteful impression on me, was, at the height of his power in the spring of '19, often accused of being a Russian Jew by the right-wing newspapers of the German Reich. In truth he was neither a Russian nor a Jew. He came from a German, Christian family residing in Moscow, had spent one part of the war on the front line with the Munich "Lifers" and another with the rear echelon in the East, had established contact early on with old university friends from Zurich among the Russian revolutionaries, and by December 1918 he was already regarded as the leader of the Munich Spartacists. An older member of the Soldiers' Council spoke after Levien. It was impossible to catch what he said; it was growing increasingly loud and increasingly hot in the room. I saw unbuttoned uniform jackets and agitated faces, and I heard private disputes here and there. Suddenly it went quiet, and everyone looked toward a side door where a small cluster of people had formed. Whispering, like orders passed down a skirmish line: "It's Eisner!" The speaker breaks off and abruptly exclaims, "Long live our prime minister, hur– ," then breaks off again before shouting "Hip, hip, hurrah!" The room and galleries roar with him. Eisner passes close by me, his sleeve brushing mine. Afterwards I have a long time to observe him from three steps away. A delicate, tiny, frail, stooped little man. His balding head is of unimposing size, his dirty gray hair hangs to the nape of his neck, his full reddish beard is turning a dirty gray, his heavy, cloudy gray eyes peer through spectacles. There is nothing brilliant, nothing venerable, nothing heroic about his entire appearance. He is a mediocre, spent man that I peg as being at least 65, although he is still in his very early fifties. He does not look especially Jewish, but he is certainly not Germanic like his opponent Levien, or Bavarian like his devotee Unterleitner. And in the way he subsequently jokes around on the podium (he does not stay behind the lectern), he does actually remind me of caricatures of Jewish journalists, of Schmock,[86] Wippchen,[87] Dr. Ulk.[88]

They announce that he has to rest for a few minutes and the discussion should continue in the meantime. This happens, and after a while he steps forward. He speaks softly and yet seems to be heard by everyone, because the room that had been so loud before is now silent, literally holding its breath. He says he just finished work and has heard nothing of what has been debated here, or perhaps leveled against him, so he can deny and refute everything. This is the first joke of many; the jokes almost always take the place of pathos for him, and they are always received with appreciative cheers. When he does resort to pathos, at least the pathos is accompanied by a dose of humor. ". . . I'm not afraid of anyone who wants to push me forward; I'm the pushiest of all, because I'm a visionary, a dreamer, a poet!" (Clamorous applause.) "I speak not as the prime minister, I speak as an Independent and a traitor. I'm supposed to ask you to vote Independent, but I'm not going to. Follow your beliefs, and let us be united!" Outbursts of cheering again and again. And then, from the heart: "Just give me a little time, I just want to be able to serve you as prime minister for a few days longer." Someone shouts from the gallery: "A hundred years!" Eisner immediately takes a bow, swinging his arm wide like a clown: "I will attempt to comply with your friendly request." And again the whole room cheers. Today I find it difficult to think of Eisner's performance as being merely comical, because it was not even a hundred days before this celebrated man, whose pure will no one could deny, lay shot on the cobblestones in front of his Residence. And yet it was absolutely and increasingly comical to witness a self-assured columnist chatter away so carelessly ("I feel like I've gotten to talking even though I didn't want to say anything"), and this columnist had toppled the Bavarian throne and was now the ruler of Bavaria, and his rapt audience – I had to keep reminding myself of this – was not a heap of literary "intellectual workers," but literally the people of Munich. Only at the end of his speech did Eisner drop the dash of humor and speak very earnestly and insistently. He called upon his listeners to go to the National Theater the following Sunday, where Andreas Latzko[89] would speak – the author of *Men in War*, the German Barbusse.[90] He said it was extremely important to listen to him, because everything depended upon "the renewal of souls." Someone like Bruno Frank could easily have said the same thing in the "council of intellectual workers," but it would hardly have garnered the same enthusiasm there as here among the thousands in the Trefler. – I had previously held the Bavarians, or at least the people of Munich, to be a fairly soulless and quite unproblematic lot; over the course of these three days, they had not become particularly more likeable to me, but certainly more puzzling. On the journey back I fell into conversation with a gentleman whose multiple dueling scars above his small goatee identified him as a former fraternity student. He was good-natured and accommodating, and I soon learned that he held a chair in Munich for some kind of forest pest studies and was currently a dean. His name was Escherich,[91] and over the next year that name would come to be known through the organization he founded, the Organization Escherich, a home guard group; but I was only with him for those few hours on the train between Munich and Regensburg and never encountered him again. Escherich spoke of Eisner without hatred, not even contemptuously – somewhat pityingly if anything. He said Eisner was a babbler with no thoughts of his own, that even as the editor of *Vorwärts* he had been incapable of writing his own feature articles, he had absolutely no future, and the upcoming man in Bavaria was already at the door: Dr. Heim,[92] the organizer of the Peasants' League, from the Center Party but not a "Black"[93] – after all, even Protestants and Jews belonged to the Peasants' League. I asked Escherich how he thought Eisner had come to power. The unsatisfactory reply was that King Ludwig[94] had brought himself to ruin and grown so unpopular on account of his Prussianization. – "How so?" – Well, in the last years of the war, the king had been obsessed with the idea of becoming "Ludwig the Increaser." He had promised to claim Strasbourg for Bavaria and, as a reward, took part in Prussian politics. The Prussians had always been Bavaria's undoing, and the people were tired of bleeding for Prussia. – "But Eisner himself is a Prussian!" – And that's precisely why he was already a dead man. – "But how did he come to power? You should have heard the thousands of people cheering for him yesterday." Escherich laughed. That was all just a bit of Munich "fun"! It would be over soon, and Munich wasn't Bavaria. He himself wanted to get away from Munich for a few days. Regensburg offered such a lovely "petrified Middle Ages." I spent hours afterward thinking about the puzzle of the Bavarian soul. They revered a mad king[95] who built extravagant fairytale castles, but they threw out a king who wanted to wangle Strasbourg for them, an "increaser," because he was involved in Prussian politics. And now, in his place, they revered a stray Prussian who built political fairytale castles of human benefaction in his speeches – "I'm a visionary, a dreamer, a poet!" Just a bit of Munich fun, Escherich had said, nothing that concerned the whole state. But could Eisner really have asserted himself and held his ground for a month and a half already solely with the support of Munich? And how much was it possible to separate the Bavarians and the people of Munich? Granted, the difference between the rural and urban population, the small town and royal capital, is very large wherever you go, and granted, it could be said in anger that the people of Munich were the degenerate part of the Bavarian peasantry – but for all that, it was absurd to try to deny the closest kinship between the one-tenth of the Bavarians in the capital and the remaining nine-tenths of the Bavarian population. The sentiment or soul of the Bavarian people was a puzzle never to be solved.

I must have been rather animated in Café Merkur as I recounted my political impressions of the time, because Harms spontaneously said: "You should write reports for us when you're in Munich." I replied just as spontaneously: "I'll sign them as your A.B. correspondent, short for Antibavaricus." We laughed and moved on to other subjects. I attached absolutely no importance to Harms's words at the time. Politics sank away again for me. Now that I would be taking on my first real German university professorship in six weeks – in Naples[96] I had, and in Ghent I would have, only taught school lessons – now I seriously had to pull myself together. The distance between accumulated material and a polished lecture is tremendous, and for your very first course of lectures, you do not leave anything to the phrasing of the moment or mere note cards. Working in the university library and making a few professional inquiries led me back to Becker and to Neubert,[97] who was newly promoted and newly wed. Neubert complained about his professor's moody and erratic nature, while Becker still treated me in the most friendly and helpful way, half paternal, half collegial. I do not want to believe the things people said of him. It is very possible that he was a somewhat fragile alcoholic, but he showed a streak of ingenuity from time to time, and quite often a certain childishness. I once found him deeply depressed. He couldn't produce anything anymore, he ran around for hours without a single thought, he was unsatisfied with the standard of his lectures – "that feeling you get when you used to be able to do something!" And for a moment he stuck out his rolled tongue like a child. I contradicted him, consoled him, and he was happy to be consoled and immediately cheered up again and talked about my work plans. – We celebrated a warm and cozy Christmas with the Scherners. It was their, or rather Hans Scherner's, belated secondary-school studies that we had to thank for two new acquaintances who would subsequently become important to us. In both cases they were people whose fates had been heavily affected by the war, but who at the moment were far too busy dealing with their private affairs to show any interest in politics. Annemarie Köhler,[98] a very sweet, fun-loving girl in her early twenties, was Scherner's fellow student, and Johannes Thieme, a starving, skinny boy of 18, was their math teacher at the cram school. Annemarie was introduced to us as the girl with the million-mark dowry. The million was hardly an exaggeration, because for generations the Köhler family had owned a large and flourishing textile mill in Crimmitschau[99] – but marriage prospects were of little concern to the robust and energetic Annemarie. She had worked as a Johanniter nurse during the war and found nursing gratifying but not entirely fulfilling, so she was now forging a path toward studying medicine. This path was certainly no longer as difficult and rarely trodden as in Ella Doehring's[100] time, but it was not yet a regular and self-evident path either. Annemarie Köhler subsequently breezed through her school exams and university studies, then became a surgical assistant at the same Johanniter hospital near Dresden where she had worked as a war nurse, before finally joining forces with a colleague[101] to open their own surgical clinic in Pirna. Throughout these years she remained in contact with us, first as a close acquaintance who popped up sporadically, then (since settling in Heidenau, and thus in our vicinity) as a cheerful, intimate friend, until finally, in these endless days of misery and persecution – I write this at the time of utmost distress, in January 1942 – she has proved to be the most faithful, indeed the only truly faithful companion in our entire circle. If I am still able to prevent myself from feeling hatred for the German people as a whole, then it is thanks solely to Annemarie's Germanness, which embodies everything I have always thought of as being German and loved for being German throughout my life. I have exactly the opposite to say about Johannes Thieme, who was presented to us as "the mathematical wunderkind." He was the son of a poor gardener's widow, had been stuck in an electrical machine factory as an apprentice mechanic with nothing more than an elementary school education, and had the misery of the war to thank for both his severe malnourishment and his advancement. He later told us how he had lain smeared with oil under a machine in the test bay and was secretly party to a scene of desperation. The manager had wanted to demonstrate a new machine to an important personage who was passing through, the head engineer in the test bay had been conscripted to serve in the army the day before despite the most urgent protests, a new man had not yet been found to take his place, and the available technicians – replacements themselves and not yet fully broken in – didn't really know what to do. So out crawled Thieme, a scrawny, grubby proletarian boy, and he said he knew the ropes – and he really did. Great astonishment on the part of the manager at the amazing autodidact, even greater on the part of Professor Punga.[102] Questions, praise, and a few words of advice and encouragement. The ambitious goal Thieme had then envisioned was a one-year[103] that could perhaps lead him to a technical school. It wasn't possible to learn everything from books alone; some instruction was needed, a few evening classes at a cram school. He had discovered two things there: first, that to "really study properly" he needed to attend a university or technical college, meaning that he needed to take an entrance exam beforehand, and second, that he could easily earn the tuition fees for the cram school by teaching math himself. He started by privately tutoring his fellow students, but the head of the cram school had soon hired him as an official teacher. He succeeded in earning his one-year very quickly, and now the majority of his compensation consisted of being able to attend all the classes for the entrance exam. He wanted to take the exam together with Scherner and Annemarie Köhler. He seemed to need just as little sleep as food; he worked eight to nine hours a day in the factory and was a student and teacher at the cram school on the side, and on top of that he had taken the exam to qualify as a journeyman mechanic. Though he looked consumptive, the doctor had declared him healthy, and he himself said he felt tough and fresh, and that once he got some peacetime food he would put on weight. We met him again in the summer of 1920 in Dresden, and he became our housemate and soon our foster son. For many years he called us Father and Mother. His area of expertise – the mathematical/technical field, in which he did make something of himself, though without ever coming close to fulfilling the expectations initially placed on him – always remained a mystery to us, but we were both able to give him various other things he needed, and he seemed to have a real affection for us. For thirteen years there was no more of a political difference between us than there was a religious or philosophical one. And then, in 1933, Thieme was the first to desert us. If, on the Day of Retribution, I could save his life with a wave of my hand, I wouldn't lift a finger. . .

Politics could only be shut out for a very short time. Over Christmas and in January there were bloody battles between Spartacus and government troops in Berlin, Noske was given dictatorial power, it looked as though at any moment the dictatorship could pass from the hands of the Social Democrats and civilians to those of a radical right-wing general, and Liebknecht and Rosa Luxemburg were murdered.[104] All of this happened on the eve of the elections to the National Assembly, and it all had a tremendous effect on the mood in Leipzig. The Independents were the strongest party there, and there was nothing in Leipzig they hated more than the *Leipziger Neueste Nachrichten*.[105] They burned the newspaper along with all sorts of reactionary leaflets in front of their community center, and unemployed workers demonstrated before the *Leipziger Neueste Nachrichten* publishing house. Kopke told me they were used to these demonstrations, which were entirely harmless; a deputation regularly appeared before the editor in chief, politely requested that a statement be printed, had it approved, and then politely withdrew. The statement then regularly appeared under the protective shield of the following sentence: "We are forced to print the following notice." But on January 17, the *Neueste Nachrichten* was forced to print and distribute a special supplement:

"We hereby condemn in the strongest possible terms the murder of Liebknecht and Rosa Luxemburg and declare that this situation could only have come to pass under the Ebert/Scheidemann government." And this time the pressure had not been brought to bear politely, but rather by raising a storm. We saw the bulk of the damage even two days later when we went to hear the first results coming in from the National Assembly election. Pictures had been shattered, lounge chairs torn up, type cases dumped out. "But they spared the big machines," Harms said, by way of consolation. "Those the German workers respect." He and Kopke had voted for the government Socialists, even though Harms, at least, stood much farther to the right than I. They had done it, they said, because now was the time to support the government – "and because the Liberals have proven incapable of governing," Harms added. In earlier years I, too, had once gone against my inner convictions and voted for the Social Democrats as a matter of pure expediency: I had wanted to support the fiercest opposition at the time. I had since matured and learned more; my immersion in Montesquieu had enriched me, and not just in philological or literary terms. Furthermore, this time it was not an election to any old house of representatives, but rather to a legislative assembly. It would have seemed like treachery to me – to both of us – to have given our vote to a cause other than liberalism. (The fact that we could vote together for the first time amplified the ceremonial nature of the scene for me. As my wife stepped behind the curtain to place her ballot in the envelope, I was reminded of my teenage infatuation with *Melitta* and *Ruth*,[106] of my sporadic enthusiasm for women's emancipation.) In later years I never again deviated from giving my vote to the Liberals, who called themselves Democrats from that point on.[107] Over and over again I heard "Their time has run out," or "They're powerless in the current situation," or "They don't have any brains in their party," – or simply "Waste of a vote." No! It was not a waste of a vote, even if some of the other objections may have been accurate. For me, the true humane world is the European world, and Europe became Europe through liberalism, and it lives on through liberalism. This is the pure and solely Europeanizing doctrine. You must pledge yourself to it, even and especially when it is powerless and disregarded.

But what became decisively important to me during these last weeks in Leipzig were neither the ceremonial moments of the National Assembly election, nor the various strikes that affected us (there were no lights at home, and the Merkur went from a café to a refuge), nor the Spartacus battles in Berlin, nor the storming of the *Leipziger Neueste Nachrichten*. The thing of decisive importance was a *Simplicissimus* caricature. It showed Erich Mühsam – whom we had both known in 1904 to be a harmlessly good-natured, entirely unpolitical bohemian and versifier in Berlin, and who was now a radical Munich politician – sitting on a red divan, getting a manicure. Underneath it said: "Manicure calluses onto my hands, I'm on the Workers' Council now!" – "That fits perfectly with your account of Eisner and the 'Council of Intellectual Workers,'" Harms said after we had laughed long enough over the picture. "You really should write reports for us from Munich." This time the comment led to a long discussion, and the old I'll-accompany-you-home, the nocturnal back-and-forth between Reichestrasse and Grassistrasse, was taken up again and practiced late into the night. I poured my heart out to Harms as if he were an older friend. I talked about my old journalistic endeavors, about my agonizing dependency on my brothers, about the uncertainty of my academic career and about my longing for an opportunity to work "above the fold"[108] for once. Harms gave me great hope. He said the new situation after the peace agreement would offer new men in journalism a chance to advance, and foreign correspondents who were familiar with the culture and character of our wartime opponents would be in demand. He elaborated on this to such an extent, and in a way so favorable to me, that on the night itself I really could imagine the publisher, Dr. Herfurth,[109] offering me the post of Paris correspondent for the *Leipziger Neueste Nachrichten* at the instigation of his lead columnist. The next day my hopes were considerably dampened. "Do you really believe," I asked directly, "that I might be considered for a post in Paris?" – "Certainly, if you settle in Paris and exploit a few

personal contacts. Maybe through your brothers? But why don't you
start by occasionally writing for us from Munich. That will give you
practice and offer you the best way in later." I was encouraged to take
the leap from another, most unexpected side as well. I traveled ahead
during our relocation to Munich in order to spend a day with my
relatives in Berlin. Posters from the election campaign for the Prussian
National Assembly[110] were still pasted to every building and monu-
ment in quantities I had never seen before. Two of them caught my
attention on account of their particular abundance and tastelessness: a
black heart with three thick, round drops spilling from it childishly –
"Who will heal the Prussian heart? The German National Party" – and
a fig leaf with the caption "The German Democratic Party is the fig leaf
for all those who dare not commit themselves to the International even
though they are Social Democrats." – I found Mother nearly blind
but exceptionally sprightly. She spoke of domestic politics with keen
interest, something she had never done before. She proudly declared
that she had voted in the National Assembly election. "Georg picked
me up in the car, but I would have gone on foot anyway – it was a
duty and an honor, after all." – "Who did you vote for, Ma?" – "The
Democrats, of course, like we all did. Only Felix voted for the government Socialists. And if it were up to him, we'd still be fighting the
French." I was not especially surprised that Georg had shifted a small
bit to the left, politically speaking, from the National Liberals to the
Liberals, nor that he had abandoned monarchism and militarism. I was
only taken aback by the rapid democratization of his social thinking.
In conversation with him, I mentioned Harms's proposal and immediately regretted it, because I feared opposition and an irritating warning
against improper associations, and I wanted to avoid all conflict. But
instead of being appalled, Georg called it an idea very much worth
considering. The time had come for political journalism on a grand
scale here, he said, while academic life was outdated and reactionary –
so if a Parisian prospect opened up for me, I should take it, and if I
needed his financial support for a time, I could be just as assured of
it in Paris as in Munich. Though of course I shouldn't give up my

professorship before I was certain of this other career path. – I wonder why I remember all of this so clearly. "Our A.B. correspondent" wrote about a dozen and a half dispatches in the following months, barely a third of which were published. The interesting middle section of the "Revolutionary Diary from the Munich Council Republic"[111] was left sitting in Dachau and did not reach Leipzig until it was completely out of date; I all but gave up writing for the newspaper at that point and grew ever more resolutely committed to my profession as a philologist. Even now, I still feel complete and undivided as a scholar and philologist. I view my *Curriculum*[112] not as a confession, but as a contribution to the intellectual and cultural history of the age. And in the midst of this current calamity, for all of my shock and desperation, I pay rapt attention to every single detail that will benefit my LTI, my *Lingua Tertii Imperii.*[113]

Why such a long prelude to this small bit of journalism on the side? I can tell you exactly why. It was then that I first heard mention of psychoanalysis and learned its technical terms, which had become fashionable. I realized very early on that, in the course of these months, I abreacted my old desire for political journalism once and for all. I proved to myself that I was capable of cooking up the professional soup I had wanted – in the Telegrams section of the *Leipziger Neueste Nachrichten* of April 11, 1919, I read: "Regarding the new turnaround in Munich, where the Independent government has fallen and (as our A.B. correspondent in Munich correctly predicted – *Ed.*) a communist government under Dr. Levien has been proclaimed. . .," and that certainly meant a diploma for A.B. – but I also found the inevitable hair (at least one) in that same soup. Deep down, however, the internal battle between the university lecturer and the journalist had already been decided in favor of the teacher on February 7, before I had even written my first article. It was on this day that I gave my first proper lecture in front of proper German students and immediately sensed a connection with them, and immediately found lecturing to be a joy and a release from everything that tormented me. And it always remained that way for seventeen years. Whatever the composition of my audience, they always went along with me. (A speaker knows precisely when this is the case, even if he is not a professor with the opportunity to verify it in seminars and exams.) And regardless of how upset or depressed I might have been when I stepped up to the lectern, after two sentences nothing existed for me besides the subject of my lecture, and after it was over I felt freer and calmer. And if the Third Reich had taken nothing more from me than the opportunity to hold lectures, it would have impoverished me enough. Nor could I ever personally understand the complaint of so many of my colleagues that lectures interfered with their own output. The best ideas for my own productive work came to me while preparing lectures, and even more often at the lectern itself, and once the idea was there I always found time to write, or at least to outline. I had been lecturing in Munich for barely fourteen days and was still very much struggling with teething problems, I was merely compiling and condensing what I found in Lotheissen[114] and Lanson[115] to use for my own purposes – and suddenly I had the notion to write my own study of Corneille,[116] and it did not leave me in peace until I began working on it.

Incidentally, if one took "proper German students" to mean the normal and conventional students at our universities, then I still had no proper students, because only soldiers returning home from the war were allowed to take part in the war emergency semester. They were older, more mature, and more feral than normal students, they had forgotten much if not all of what they had learned in school and previous university semesters, they wanted to catch up and progress as quickly as possible, many were intellectually starved, a good many – most, in fact – faced economic hardship, and all of them longed to be finished with their studies. They had to be taught with more focus, and you had to wrest their attention more directly and decisively than is necessary under normal circumstances. They had been torn from their student life by great affairs of state; I introduced them to French Classicism by first telling them how the pulse of the state beat through all of these works and only then addressing the ways in which the content was expressed, the aesthetics. Less enjoyable than these lectures were the preparatory courses for the matriculation exam, which were held with groups of twenty-five students. There was not a single philologist among them in my classes – governments everywhere were warning against this discipline, as their supply of candidates for teaching positions at secondary schools was covered for years; most of the students wanted to be doctors, or even dentists or veterinarians, with a few hoping for something in economics. They were naturally interested solely in their chosen subject, and having to make up the matriculation exam was considered an embarrassing and useless formality. At the very least, they did not want to sacrifice any time to working on it at home – the lecturers should just see what they could drum into them, and then they would see if some examiner had the nerve to let decorated war heroes and old students fail a childish school exam! What could one do in the face of such an attitude, with no disciplinary authority? We had to be pleased if even half of the twenty-five showed up, and if just a few of these dozen students expressed some willingness to work. I can say "we" in good conscience, because all of my colleagues teaching these classes had exactly the same complaints. I myself sometimes wondered if I encountered more dire deficiencies in the French class or the German one. In French the mistakes were more glaring and primitive – several times I heard *je suis nu* instead of *je suis né*[117] – while in German they were more embarrassing and depressing. My instructions were to expose the examinees to German literature from the *Sturm und Drang* period to Goethe's death, to have them give class lectures and write essays in this area – no one was to be admitted to the final exam without proof of such essays and presentations. About the only good thing I have to say of my people is that they had a command of spelling and grammar. But they had shockingly little to say, either orally or in writing, about *The Robbers*, or *Carlos*, or *Wallenstein*.[118] And between their meager sentences, there always seemed to be a listless protest: "Why do I have to concern myself with this? I just want to fill teeth." As it transpired, it truly would have been useless for the course participants to concern themselves with it, because when the urgent call went out for Freikorps recruits in the summer, every student who joined was exempted from having to make up the matriculation exam. That was the case in Munich, anyway. It is unlikely to have been different anywhere else. Later on in Dresden, I had ample opportunity to further experience the educational background and general literacy of the student body after the war. In Munich, I did not yet take the issue too seriously; I thoroughly sympathized with the poor boys and couldn't blame them for their reluctance and restlessness – and I also didn't have the time to ponder the potential consequences of a lower level of general education among academics. Between lectures, I tended to haunt the work room for several hours. I had first visited it as a candidate lecturer, and even then I felt I had been lifted above the mass of students who were reliant on the general reading room. Now I experienced a second advancement. The work room was divided into two lengthwise: privileged academics sat on the window side, while the remaining faculty members sat on the inside. Each lecturer had a table with his own shelf where he could stack his books and leave them overnight. Additionally, on the professors' side, anything you requested from the library was immediately delivered to you by special runners. And there was yet another advantage attached to this side, though one which I later – from about the summer onward – found to be a distressing disadvantage: you were forever elbow to elbow with your colleagues. If Muncker or Vossler or some other bigwig wasn't inquiring benevolently about the progress of my work or whispering something about the last faculty meeting, then someone of equal rank and age was pulling me into the corridor to discuss some problem or other over a few drags on a cigar. I was initially pleased to move closer to my circle of colleagues in this way; after all, I was going to spend the next five years as a university lecturer in Munich and I knew very few members of the faculty. Later, in the tremendous confusion of the political situation, I felt the constant urge to hear this or that opinion on the state of things. In the third and longest phase of this period in Munich, however, I mostly found these collegial conversations to be a very unwelcome interruption. I could certainly have frequented a calmer place to work at the university: the Romance Philology department. The few students who sat there were quiet as a mouse in the presence of a lecturer, and I had the richest assortment of specialist literature to hand. Why didn't I relocate? I tried to convince myself that I wouldn't have access to the supporting material I needed for my German classes in that pure Romance environment. But deep down, I knew right from the start what made that quiet, spacious place disagreeable to me. It was the monstrous abundance of academic literature, grammar books, dictionaries, old journals, and hefty specialist biographies that oppressed me. "Outsider! Outsider!" these full shelves shouted at me. The few industrious students there availed themselves of all these resources with ease, while I, the university lecturer, had to laboriously orient myself, and every attempt at orientation reminded me of the gaps in my professional knowledge. Granted, when I was feeling fresh, I would tell myself, "Your Montesquieu is worth something, and your lectures, too; you're producing on your own terms, and if you need material, you work for it." But in the Romance Philology department I felt suffocated by the mass of unfamiliar specialist material, as if I were buried under a tombstone. There was a third place I could use between lectures, the professors' room. But all too often I fell victim to Lerch there. We met often anyway, of course, but while it was interesting to chat with him everywhere else, he regularly got on my nerves terribly there. This is because the professors' room held the complaints book. You could use this book to complain that it had been drafty in the lecture hall, or too hot or too cold, or anything else of that nature, and Lerch always had something to complain about. I once found him indignant – the complaints book wasn't in its usual place. "What will you do now?" I asked him. "The blotter has been left here," he replied seriously, "Look, I've written in big letters, 'Complaint: moving the complaints book from its usual place is not permitted!'" But once he had started complaining, he inevitably fell to impugning the skills of the Romance philology lecturers, which robbed me of all courage.

In terms of distance, I could have worked at home instead of the university without losing any time, but when it came to peace and quiet, that was often a case of jumping from the frying pan into the fire. After another promptly unsuccessful attempt to find our own apartment, we had quickly taken accommodation in a boarding house. The house at Schellingstrasse 7 was across from the side wing of the university and separated from Ludwigstrasse only by a corner build-ing. When we leaned out the window we could just see the entrance to the Ministry of War, a sight that became significant in the coming weeks. When it came to boarding houses, we now had the appropriate measure of experience and resignation. We expected it to be tolerable and knew from the outset that it would become intolerable after a while. We lived tolerably for nearly a full year with Frau Konradine Berg, the youthful Munich grandmother with the naughty, stentori-ously reared little granddaughter of uncertain origin, and when at last there was friction, it was not so much the fault of the landlady herself as the brutal price increase. We got on well with our fellow lodgers and external dinner guests, though we never formed as close a group as we had in Leipzig. Nonetheless, our sitting room, which was connected to a small bedroom, was so popular that I had no more assurance of being able to work uninterrupted there than over in the work room. This popularity was based partly on the piano we had had delivered from the furniture storehouse, partly on the letter scale that graced our desk. Of the two instruments, the letter scale was by far the more important at the time, both in itself and from the viewpoint of con-temporary history. No one was satiated by the boarding house food, of course; the old wartime misery of stamps for groceries had certainly not ended with the cease-fire (and, in fact, it continued long after the peace agreement), and the search for suppliers and foraging trips were still commonplace. Group buying and bartering undoubtedly flour-ished just as much in other boarding houses as they did in ours. I can honestly say "in ours," because this business was regularly conducted in our sitting room, and whatever bacon, butter, cheese, or choco-late was owed to someone would be weighed on the letter scale. It could weigh up to 1,000 grams – and who could have afforded larger quantities? The weighing and apportioning was always accompanied by chatter, and it always took precedence over French Classicism and counterpoint exercises, which is why my wife would try to spend her days at the music academy or the Protestant church, while I favored the work room. Of the many people we came into contact with at the boarding house, only three left a definite impression on me. A lasting affinity formed between us and the tall Dr. Ritter[119] on the very first day. He was about five years younger than us, had served as a doctor in the war and was now assisting the famous Sauerbruch,[120] whom he said was the most important surgeon in Germany. He was a Catholic Rhinelander, and I found his attitude toward Catholicism to be the strangest thing about him. He made no attempt to conceal the easygoing worldliness of his nature. "Live well" – by which he meant "eat well" – was one of his favorite expressions. "We're going to live well again," he would say when bacon was weighed in our room, and he himself handled the division of group spoils as seriously as if it were a surgical procedure. But he was even more passionately devoted to his profession than to "living well," and we were probably both so well disposed toward him because we enjoyed hearing his accounts of being a doctor. His fervent wish for the future was to be allowed to run a hospital himself someday. "It won't happen with science and practical competence alone," he said candidly. "Connections are essential, maybe the most important thing. I'm currently in the same Catholic academics' association as our Archbishop Faulhaber,[121] and I'm hoping for the nurse route a bit as well." I asked him what that was. Well, when it came to allocating management positions in municipal and association hospitals, the head nurses often had a very important say in the matter, so it was good to be in their favor. He said this in neither a scheming, nor self-seeking, nor cynical way, he merely noted it with the clearest conscience and perfect contentment. "As a doctor, isn't it sometimes hard to stay on friendly terms with the nurses?" – "Not in the least. There are no better nurses than our Catholic sisters, and you can really trust the judgment of an old matron." I thought of my experiences in Paderborn.[122] "Don't you sometimes feel constricted by the priority given to religion?" – "Never, on the contrary! It supports us, it's good for the patients, it calms them. And as for myself," he added simply, "I always like to hear the nurses praying." – "Can you reconcile your faith with your scientific knowledge?" – "Easily. Why should there be any friction? As a doctor I deal with nature, and as a Catholic I deal with the supernatural, or the creator of nature. I believe what my parents believe, and all of my relatives and teachers, and I can't even imagine my life without this belief." He put all of this forth as a matter of the utmost self-evidence, and he was very clearly just as surprised by my surprise as I was by his frame of mind. Of course, this talk of religion was an exception in our discussions. The "good life," Sauerbruch, operations, his warm-hearted interest in his patients (and not just their conditions), a bit of politics (tending toward the Center) – these were the usual subjects. And then there was something that went beyond all of this for him, even beyond medicine, and at least periodically filled his cheerful soul with melancholy: he had a great but not very happy love of music. He sang with a good deal of artistic appreciation and effort, but his trained voice was only a small (even for the purposes of singing at home) and brittle tenor. He was aware of the deficiency, and sometimes, after he had attended a concert, he would sigh, "If only I had such a voice." But then he would immediately turn to my wife and say, "Shall we try *Winter Journey*[123] again this evening? It's so beautiful!"

Ritter's even temper stood in the starkest contrast to that of Arnold Weissberger,[124] a student about ten years younger. The two got along, incidentally. Ritter bantered good-naturedly, and Weissberger was far too intelligent not to recognize the innocent nature of the banter. He had enormous, rheumy, blazing black Jewish eyes in a pallid face, and while his outward bearing was always composed, he blazed on the inside just like his eyes. He was drawn to literature and philosophy, he grappled with metaphysical problems, and it was only in deference to the will of his father[125] that he studied chemistry, so he could take over his father's factory in Chemnitz one day. We stayed in close contact with Ritter and Weissberger for many years. Ritter reached his desired goal, probably by way of the nurse route and certainly for the good of his patients: he became a hospital director in Regensburg. While still in Munich, Weissberger developed a liking for the chemistry that had been forced upon him – such a great liking that he never did take over his father's factory. He devoted himself entirely to science. When the Third Reich swept in, he was just about to habilitate in Leipzig.[126] He was able to escape to Cambridge. The untroubled Ritter and the uneasy Weissberger were timeless characters, so to speak; their contrary expressions of humanity would have appealed to me always and anywhere. Pontius, on the other hand, was of interest to me only as a contemporary phenomenon. To this day I cannot say exactly what kind of person he was. Hans Meyerhof simply called him a washerwoman, and this was fitting, because the man was wishy-washy and softish and talkative and gossipy – but that didn't explain him. Everything about Pontius, his background, his profession, his character, his ethos, were and remained obscure to us. He had been born in Russia, studied chemistry in Zurich without graduating, fought on the front line as a Bavarian, and served as an interpreter during the peace negotiations in Brest-Litovsk. His family, a wife and child, were now living in the occupied Rhineland and could not join him. He told us all of this. But which parts of it were true? What was he living on in Munich? We met him in the company of Hans Meyerhof the day before he came to our boarding house as a lunch guest. He attached himself to us in a more than affectionate way. He sat on our sofa for hours, even when we paid no attention to him. He liked to confess, and sometimes he dissolved into floods of tears over his failed life. He was a good storyteller. He was a talented illustrator. He once drew very accurate caricatures of everyone around the table, had the portraits photographed together on a single sheet, and distributed the sheets. Where did he get the money from? He didn't seem to be involved in smuggling. Was he a political agent? He seemed too careless for that, too uncontrolled, and too good-natured. In the time that followed, I never saw him do anyone harm nor come into means himself. But he always kept his head above water, and later on his family showed up.

He spent hours playing chess in Café Stephanie with Levien, and back at the boarding house he called Levien the most depraved creature. In the summer he served for a while in the Freikorps Wolf[127] – "Wages of 19 marks a day, and I'm free to quit on a week's notice – why shouldn't I take it?" – The Freikorps were growing more radically right-wing and anti-Jewish by the day, and afterward Pontius sat comfortably with us, and with Hans on Barer Strasse, and he said to me with genuine sadness: "You mustn't pin your hopes on Dresden,[128] they're so anti-Semitic there." – "What does that have to do with me? I'm Protestant." – "But people know your family, and they go by your ancestry, not your denomination . . ." Pontius always remained a mystery to me. When we left the Berg boarding house in early 1920, we lost sight of him, and I never heard from him again. – I met with Hans every day, and we had no political clashes in these first weeks of February because he was heartily devoted to Eisner, and anyone who championed Eisner was considered a moderate centrist at the time. The wisdom of my first A.B. dispatch[129] was actually thanks entirely to my interactions with Hans. I was continually occupied by the connection between Munich politics and the Munich bohemians. The distribution of votes in the newly elected state assembly was not favorable to Eisner.[130] Despite this, I said, he could hold his ground as prime minister – and not just because the bourgeoisie considered him the lesser evil compared to Levien and Mühsam, but because this very same Levien and Mühsam, for all that they feuded with him so fiercely, spared him nonetheless. "They won't seriously attack him," I wrote at the end of the article, "They feel too much affinity with him for that. They are hostile brothers, but they are brothers all the same – in bohemianism."

Two Munich Ceremonies

[Munich, in early February 1919]

Two ceremonies, two worlds! And how easy it would be for an independent to pit the simple, truthful, purely idealist, despicably misunderstood new world against the old, empty world of base pretense! Thursday, February 6th, in the large concert hall of the Odeon, decorated solely with the cold, massive metal pipes of the organ: the memorial service of the Munich U.S.P.[131] for Karl Liebknecht, Rosa Luxemburg and Franz Mehring.[132] The performers who promised songs and an organ recital fail to appear, so the martyrs are honored before the modest crowd only with a speech by Gustav Landauer,[133] a slight man in a black coat with the black mane and tone of a prophet. Then on Sunday, February 8th, in the magnificent auditorium of the university, a magnificent celebration for the academic participants in the war who were now returning to peacetime work. The splendor of the *ancien régime*: the brown, fiery red, carmine, deep blue and black of the professors' gowns, the rector's golden chain of office, the golden staves of the advancing beadles, students in full gala dress, white and green and red, with fabulous riding boots and fencing blades, with ribbons and banners. And a wealth of the finest music ... The world of truth against the world of pretense!

Really?

The romantic Gustav Landauer, who referred to himself as an unpolitical politician, actually only talked about his personal friend Karl Liebknecht. Mehring, who no longer knew the real hunger of the proletariat, merely served as an introduction. He had written two different stories of social democracy because there were two different social democracies: the one pure, idealistic – the other materialistic, militaristic, sergeant-majorish, even amenable to general staff officers, to men from the "war of shame"! Dead Rosa was only touched upon as well, held up solely as Liebknecht's loyal comrade, even though she had actually been the only real man in her party. But as for Liebknecht himself! The man of will, of action, of the creative idea, who had overcome the softness within himself in order to be fully effective. Who was a successor to Luther – to whom his family traced back their genealogy –, who had been an earthly savior, and who was martyred as such. Oh, if only there had still been brave men in Germany in 1916! (This was received placidly by the assembled listeners, hundreds of whom had probably stood before the enemy in 1916.) Then, in accordance with Liebknecht's idea, the war would

have been ended, the world benefacted. But now that everything had turned out so differently, there was only one form of world benefaction and "salvation" that would simultaneously be an atonement and memorial for the "murdered" Liebknecht: the Council Republic, the true republic instead of the Weimar lie . . .

This is what the truth looked like on Thursday in the Odeon. And on Sunday at the university, Rector Clemens Baeumker, the Catholic philosopher, friend and colleague of the late Hertling,[134] essentially covered the same ground: an overview of the events from 1914 until today. How different it all sounded. And yet not contrary or anti-revolutionary in the usual sense! The enthusiasm of 1914 resounded once more and was not disparaged, the courage of the soldiers outside was not forgotten. With grave words, the speaker then recalled the abrupt collapse. An arresting image: just as Zeppelin had reached Echterdingen[135] and then crashed and shattered to pieces, Germany had done the same. And there should be no vilification of those who had fallen, but rather words of respect for all who had struggled and stood the test at the highest levels under the old regime. But also no words of accusation against the new age. It had to come, and we intellectuals should not stand in its way or try to bring back the dead. However (spoken as a philosopher before university students), we hold fast to the immanence of that past life in the present, to its continued development, its continued effect. . .

So, where is the world of pretense and where the world of truth? In the distortive phrases spoken in the Odeon, or the deliberative words in the university auditorium?

Stranger even than the contrast between the two speakers, however, was their agreement; they both ended with one and the same beseeching claim: we have to work if we want to be saved. The only question now is who points to the better way of working, the people of the Odeon or the others; the people of the always-intangible International or the ones who profess their devotion to Germany, to a whole Germany, one in which the academics, with their welcoming telegram sent to German-Austrian universities, explicitly include German-Austria.

A.B.

Hans spoke to me often about his dealings with leading politicians, but the only person I ever saw him with, other than business acquaintances, was a journalist from Württemberg named Weckerle,[136] a man who was even more embittered and radical than Hans, but who also sympathized with Eisner. I asked if there might be an opportunity for me to meet Eisner personally. "Sure," Hans said, "I'll invite you over together." I thought he was joshing, but on the morning of February 19th he came to the boarding house. "The Eisners are having coffee at my place this evening, why don't you drop by?" We were somewhat disappointed, as only Frau and Fräulein Eisner were present. The daughter, from his first marriage, was a robust, red-haired girl, while his second wife[137] was a gentle, youthful creature. Both ladies appeared very modest, without any pretensions. Though Frau Eisner spoke of her husband in an effusive manner, she did so not as someone who

venerates a powerful statesman, but as someone who cherishes a pastor
and adores an apostle. He was sacrificing himself for his office, she said;
even now it had not been possible to tear him from his work. But his
devotion was rewarded; no one who heard him speak for even just a few
minutes could resist him, rough peasants and jaundiced strikers alike
had wept at his words. I thought about the gibing journalists and found
Frau Eisner's effusiveness odd; I thought about the recent cheering of
the thousands, about the rapturous "Over my dead body!" uttered by
the sturdy Unterleitner, and I could not entirely disagree with Frau
Eisner. I told her how much I would have liked to meet her husband
in private at some point. Since I was friends with Hans that was sure
to happen, she replied; "My husband likes Herr Meyerhof very much,
and he's certain to make up for the visit he promised today." A day and
a half after this get-together, at noon on Friday the 21st, I was working
on my lecture in the work room when the door was yanked open so
loudly that everyone looked up, and an attendant took a few steps into
the center aisle and shouted in an agitated voice: "Please stop working
and leave the building, the university is closing immediately – the
prime minister has been assassinated." There was a commotion and
volley of questions. The attendant didn't know much: orders from the
rector's office, if the gentlemen would just leave quickly so the building
could be closed – Eisner was said to have been shot openly in the street
by a corps student,[138] and the hand grenade that had recently been
thrown at the State Parliament was also attributed to a corps student, so
the university and technical college really had "nothing to laugh about"
now. I heeded my calling as an A.B. man and made my way through
the city. Stores and restaurants were already closed, and the circular
clusters of people I had first noticed in December had already formed
everywhere. A very long procession of workers, uniformed men, and
adolescents marched down Ludwigstrasse. There were shouts of "To
the Theresienwiese!" and "Vengeance for Eisner!" but they did not
sound overly agitated, and no one was carrying weapons. The city took
on a more threatening appearance as trucks arrived, red flags fluttering
from them, crammed full of standing soldiers holding their weapons at

the ready or ostentatiously loading them. But no shots were fired. On the Theresienwiese, too, it remained relatively quiet. Apparently not too many demonstrators had shown up, and in such a huge space[139] even a few thousand shrunk into a small group. This relative calm contrasted with the ferocity of the leaflets that were soon distributed. They called for the suppression of the bourgeois press, for a general strike, for a "second revolution." I went to Hans and found him with the journalist Weckerle and two men I didn't know, who were introduced to me as members of the Workers' Council. All of them were terribly grim, Weckerle most of all, whose face suddenly seemed haggard and whose eyes blazed. He spoke in choppy words: "vengeance" . . . and "bourgeois hostages" and "dictatorship of the proletariat" and "Council Republic." Everyone agreed that the Council Republic would be proclaimed tomorrow or the day after, and that all power would now fall to Levien. The State Parliament with its bourgeoisie would slink away.

Munich After Eisner's Assassination

(From our A.B. correspondent)

Munich, Febr. 22 [1919]

The living and the dead Eisner. – The "second revolution." – Count, corps student and officer. – Painful uncertainty. – The cityscape. – The "Lifers." – On the Theresienwiese. – The unsettling airplanes. – The violated freedom of the press. – The vanished State Parliament. – Auer.[140]

It is trivial to say that, aside from all moral reprehensibility, political murder is foolish; and trivial to say there's a fool born every minute. But even in these past months, there has been no more of an infuriatingly senseless act than Eisner's murder. No one doubted Eisner's entirely pure intentions. He wanted nothing for himself; although the abruptness of his ascent had naturally filled him with self-assurance, he had none of the excruciating vanity of Karl Liebknecht or the bloody fanaticism of Rosa Luxemburg. He wanted to keep his hands clean of money, and of blood. He always had the best will, and when dealing with others – particularly those in the Entente camp, who are so remarkably skilled at wrapping a semblance of humanity around the most brutal desire for power – he assumed the same innocence of spirit (just look at Bern!).[141] This is why he was so politically contested, this is why – as I recently described – he managed to stay upright, in all of his innocence, under the pressure of the parties on the Right and Left. He floated, in fact, since the solid ground had long been pulled out from under him, and since he did not know what to do with solid ground anyway, and this is why the dead Eisner now

has infinitely more followers than the living one ever did. Some say that he is a martyr, others that he is pitiable, and most think that with him – the living Eisner – and probably above and beyond him, the situation could have calmed down very quickly, that the State Parliament would have settled in, forcibly assumed authority and soon put a more reasonable government in place.

Now, however . . . The mood is Descartes-esque. The only certainty is that everything is in doubt. It is still quiet, or what passes for quiet in these sorry times. Quiet apart from a few nightly shootings, a few occupied editorial offices and the usual strikes, to which the Bavarian is all the more eager to submit ever since the southern abundance of Catholic holidays was taken from him. But what the next hours will bring no one knows; and whatever they bring, the uncertainty will remain, and the ugly rallying cry of the "second revolution" that was immediately tossed into the agitated crowd yesterday has taken on sinister life. A large poster has been pasted to the advertising columns with a few very canny words from *Fechenbach*,[142] the private secretary of the deceased. "Eisner's Legacy" is the headline, and the poster calls on all Social Democrats to unite. If this unification takes place, it will certainly be *under the leadership of the radical elements*; if it does not, then the fissures and the uncertainty will be even greater. The bourgeoisie is quite helpless at the moment. It was a "count" who shot the unbloody Eisner, and he is said to be a corps student as well. Count and corps student and officer and capitalist and bourgeois – it's all one and the same now, there's no time for finer distinctions. Unfortunately, it must also be said that the student corps has behaved in a most unpleasant and provocative way here, and it has at least as many opponents at the university, even among lecturers and students, as the Independent Social Democrats have among the government Socialists. However – and this is also characteristic of the current situation – I can only write that the murderer is "*said* to be" a corps student. Whether he actually was, or whether he is still alive, is just as much a mystery to the public here as *Auer*'s condi-

tion or to whom the assassination attempt on Auer[143] should be attributed. The vengeance of the Independents – the reactionaries want to do away with the government entirely – senseless act of a lone embittered Eisner supporter . . . You hear all of this and much more, and everyone lives in uncertainty.

The entire cityscape was changed yesterday in a single blow. Before you even knew what had happened, you sensed the effects. Suddenly the streetcars stopped running, stores and restaurants closed, and students streamed out of the university and technical college, which were shut down immediately until Monday. The hand grenade recently thrown at the State Parliament is also being quite confidently attributed to a corps student, so the university in particular "really has nothing to laugh about" now. Then you saw a long, long line of workers, adolescents, and men in uniform crossing Ludwigstrasse. There were shouts of "To the Theresienwiese!" – "Vengeance for Eisner!" – "Down with the Blacks!" – but on the whole it was a strangely quiet and sober procession. The public rather gloomily watched them pass. They are "still unarmed," as you heard often enough, with ominous emphasis on the word "still." Then the curious *circular clusters of people* that are perhaps peculiar to Munich began to form on the streets and squares. Somewhere in the center of the cluster something is said or explained, not especially loudly, and the cluster revolves around the center and asks what's happening. Five steps away there is a second, equally symmetrical cluster, then a third, a sixth, a twelfth. . . . One shot would be enough to merge these groups, turning them into a chaotic mass. I was surprised all day long that this shot was never fired, because very soon trucks arrived crammed full of standing soldiers, each of them holding his weapon at the ready, some loading their weapons more ostentatiously than cautiously. Machine guns were mounted on the vehicles as well. But the main thing was the big red flags: some of them plain red, some with writing, one even with the Turkish crescent, but it was such a lovely red that the crescent was not distracting. The people cheered, and at times you could well have forgotten the seriousness of the affair and thought of it as *a carnival amusement*. The Lifeguards sat merrily on the windowsills in the Türkenkaserne,[144] dangling their legs, joking with passers-by. The Lifeguards are considered to be practically monarchist, and they are being quartered with some of the sailors who undertook the dark putsch "for the protection of the State Parliament"[145] a few days ago. "Have you been locked up?" their laughing comrades shouted up at them in passing. "Nah!" came the equally cheerful reply. . . . Flyers called for vengeance and for a second revolution and for an assembly on the Theresienwiese, but they also announced a meeting of the Workers' and Soldiers' Council in the Deutsches Theater.

Perhaps this is what divided the people's interest, because despite the glorious spring weather, which revealed the delicate line of the Alps on the horizon, it was not overly busy around the Bavaria statue; of course, the *Theresienwiese* can swallow up such tremendous numbers of people that even a few thousand look like just a small heap. It was in such a modest crowd that I saw a sailor standing on the simplest of stages later in the afternoon. He shouted in a powerful voice. Individual calming words were audible, such as "not quite a bloodbath – but confinement – officers – reactionaries – murderers . . ." The goings-on in the city itself were actually much more lively and threatening than on the Theresienwiese. In front of the *München-Augsburger Zeitung*, which was already occupied, soldiers swung their hand grenades, and posters called for the occupation of the entire bourgeois press (which was made responsible for everything) and for a general strike. And everywhere there were throngs of people, everywhere the ominous, inflammable automobiles. Finally, as the sun went down, there came an aesthetic diversion, a lovely, temporary conclusion to the affair: half a dozen *airplanes* suddenly appeared over the square in front of the Sendlinger Gate. They glinted and gleamed against the bright blue sky, made the most daring turns, performed the most wonderful nosedives and loops, now grazing the rooftops, now ascending to fabulous heights; and everywhere they released masses of flyers (only now really earning their name), which looked like flocks of white doves catching the sun and, as they drifted down, really did bring a sort of pacification with them: an appeal for calm, the announcement of martial law, and an order to leave the streets at seven o'clock.

It did grow quieter then, and the streets emptied . . . But there were shots and looting in the night (even yesterday people could be seen gathering in front of this or that villa where "they've got food in the cellar"), assemblies are already meeting early today, everyone is on strike, the mail and newspapers have stopped, the workers are arming themselves . . . And the only certainty is uncertainty.

*

Postscript. At the train station they said "with this whole lark" they didn't know when a letter would reach Leipzig, so on the off chance, I am sending a few additions to the dispatch from this morning.

When I was being trained for the field here, I had to spend some

Sundays moping in the barracks; the garrison would be confined because some soldier had gone for his knife during a brawl. Now I am confined again, along with the entire population, at least from 7 o'clock in the evening onward, and I am just as innocent now as I was then. The fanaticism of a single person has brought this upon me, just as the alcoholism of a single person did back then. . . In place of the suppressed bourgeois newspapers, we have "Volume One, Number One" – one for all – of the "Newsletter of the Central Committee," which rejects the assertion that *Auer* fell victim to an act of revenge by the Spartacists and believes that "the type of murderous, Noske-style butchery that was carried out in Berlin, Bremen and elsewhere" is an impossibility in Munich.

We should actually be content; the day has been quiet, posters on the walls warn that looters and thieves will be shot, and the weapons of the workers that are meant to defend the revolution have not been used anywhere, because no opponents could be found. (But that's just the cowardice of the bourgeoisie and reactionaries, of course!) And we have a newspaper again, which (apparently drawing on older material) even published the death notice of a corps student with the corps monogram.

And yet, anyone who does not take a very, and I mean very, pig-headed view of the situation must be in a bad enough humor. No one here knows where the *State Parliament* has gone. I spoke to three members of the Workers' Council. One said it had crawled off somewhere, another said "We'll throw them out," and the third said "We're all united, even the Peasants' Council; as of today there is only a Bavarian Council Republic!" And they all said there were no Majority Socialists here, no Independents or Spartacists anymore, just a united proletariat, and its eleven-man committee[146] – which includes Dr. Levien – reigns supreme. So unification, in this case, means the hegemony of the extreme Left. You may wonder how many Bavarians (who, after all, elected a very different State Parliament!) stand behind this dictatorship of the proletariat, and you may also wonder how the National Assembly, how the

Reich, is supposed to respond to this Council Republic, which will make a mockery of democracy. A mockery of freedom! After all, *the bourgeois press has already been suppressed* and the humane government is already resorting to *protective custody* "to protect the bourgeoisie from the beast that the bourgeoisie itself let loose." I want to quote once again from this same oral source: "We'll smoke out the mob, we must demand hostages." Knowing well the mood at the university, I retorted that if the student corps showed the least bit of solidarity with the perpetrator or his views, they would have no more bitter enemies than those within the university itself. The reply: Why did the student body never stand up for Eisner? – What can you say to that? This is the kind of judgment that the current ruling party passes on whole groups, on all groups that are not part of the proletariat itself. And that party feels justified and strong because it has a martyr. Incidentally, people only speak of Auer in passing – he is still alive, they say, and then: he always conspired against Eisner!

Today when I read the dispatch I wrote for the *Leipziger Neueste Nachrichten*[147] while these impressions were fresh in my mind, I'm actually surprised that they published it, because it scarcely fits with their reactionary substance. Granted, I viewed the looming dominion of the Spartacists as senseless slavery and also did not think much of Eisner's statesmanship. But I very heavily emphasized the absolute integrity of his intentions, the fact that his hands were clean of both money and blood. I referred to the murder committed by Count Arco,[148] who very quickly began to be glorified by the Right, as "infuriatingly senseless," and I referred to the behavior of the student corps, to which the count was said to belong, as "most unpleasant and provocative." When I added that the majority of students and lecturers utterly objected to this behavior, it was not only my honest belief at the time, it was also probably still true at that moment. Only in the coming months did attitudes change. In the event, Eisner's assassination was not immediately followed by the Munich Council Republic. Instead, a gradually deteriorating interim state held sway into early April. There were strikes, the bourgeois newspapers were suppressed, occasionally there was shooting, occasionally a villa would be looted; but a certain degree of movement was still possible among the moderates and the parties on the Right, an actual dictatorship of the proletariat had not yet been achieved, and open war was not yet being waged with the Reich – or, as people put it, with "Weimar." I took a break from journalism in this interim. For a while I lacked an external impetus, because the Leipzig press had been stymied by a general strike, and for a while I was very much occupied with a severe illness my wife had contracted. It started as a harmless tooth abscess but quickly escalated to a nasty sepsis. Our next-door neighbor, Leo Ritter, proved to be most compassionate in this situation. He would be on hand half the night to help out. I was so concerned that it was a struggle to fulfill my lecturer's duties. Furthermore, the most I could manage were notes in my diary, certainly not a well-formed study. My wife was not back on her feet until the end of March; we believed she had pulled through unscathed, and my head was clearer. None of this is to say that, in the alternating surroundings of the hospital room and the university, I had entirely forgotten politics. It never allowed itself to be forgotten, it infiltrated and dominated everything. When Ritter visited my wife, he talked about Count Arco's condition and the efforts of the Spartacists to have him imprisoned. The assassin himself had been shot on the spot by a sentry and was now lying on the verge of death in Sauerbruch's clinic. Sauerbruch refused to release him, and the brusquer the Spartacists became, the more the bourgeoisie, and particularly the students, glorified the count as their hero. Whenever I went over to the university I saw the red flag flying from its roof, and its entryways had been closed to a slit; no one entered without identification. It goes without saying that the discussions inside and outside the work room revolved around politics, but now politics found its way into the lecture hall as well, just as it had in 1915 in Naples. I had assigned presentations in my exam preparation class. A young man stood up at attention: "Lieutenant Strasser."[149] (It was most unusual to mention one's military rank here.

Incidentally, the very young man spoke without any vocal effort or particular emphasis.) "I took the topic of Goethe's youth, after 'Truth and Poetry.'[150] Would the professor permit me to speak instead about the nature and goals of the Spartacus League? It is so essential to enlighten my fellow students." There was immediately a very fierce rustle of disapproval; it was clear that hardly anyone present sympathized with the Spartacus League. I asked for silence and said roughly the same thing (but less emotionally) that I had said to the students in Naples: we should leave politics aside here and work. It was well received; Strasser sat down again without objection and I was able to continue. After the lecture he came to my desk and asked if he could explain his views to me. "Certainly – just not in class. Walk with me." He said he had fought in the war as an Austrian volunteer, and he had emphasized his officer's rank earlier because, in general, the officers leaned to the Right. He thought it was necessary to talk about the Spartacus League especially here at the university because the students were proving more and more reactionary by the day. He was convinced that the reign of communism was not to be stopped, that only communism was capable of offering salvation for all. . . I interrupted him and said that I personally would not be swayed from my moderate position and was averse to any form of extremism, and as a teacher I had to ensure that my classroom hours were spent on the actual subject of instruction. He took his leave and was not seen in the German class any more. But I was to encounter his name again. In order to visit Vossler with Lerch one evening, I had to pick up a pass from the police station because we were forbidden to be on the streets after 7 o'clock. After much consideration and hesitation, the pass was finally issued to me "for the purposes of an academic meeting"; it was actually only supposed to be given to doctors and midwives. I rather welcomed the political talk during this meeting, because when I was alone with Vossler and Lerch, I felt as though I were facing a merciless, hostile superior power in the field of philology; I only went along to avoid finding myself in the embarrassing position of aggrieved marginalization. Politically speaking, there were absolutely no stark differences between us. In general, I still believed that I was largely in harmony with my academic and bourgeois surroundings. Even two very unpleasant incidents during the awkward inaugural visits had not especially given me pause. These inaugural visits, which went on all through 1919 and never ended! The faculty had over 70 members, and it was considered the duty of each newcomer (and certainly each novice and lecturer) to visit all of them, all ideally on a Sunday morning, all in a frock coat and top hat, married men together with their wives, single men and widowers alone. Lerch and I talked long and inconclusively about the case of Jordan (whose wife was in a mental hospital). On the Sunday before my wife was laid low, we were only able to make two calls because we were received both times. We first called on the Anglicist and privy councilor Schick, whom I had heard lecture back in 1902.[151] His wife[152] – a gray-haired Englishwoman who, after several decades in Munich, spoke fluent German but with a penetrating English accent – received us in her husband's absence with overflowing, intensely pastoral warmth. She grasped my wife by both hands and pulled her close on the plush sofa. "We women" had to stick together now, she said, to heal the wounds of the war; there could no longer be English or German or French women, just women, just women and wives. And did we really think the English had wanted the war? They'd had as little appetite for blood as the Germans or the French – no, no one had this slaughter on their conscience but the Jews alone, who were the only ones to profit from it. We stared at the old woman in silent bewilderment; she took it for sympathy and preached on about the sisterly bond between all female hearts. We had hoped to get six visits out of the way on this Sunday (you handed over the visiting card, and the well-trained servant girl would say, "My master and mistress will be very sorry to have missed you"), and the next in line were the Joachimsens,[153] a married couple of middling years. The husband, a scholar of early modern history, was known to be a German nationalist. The talk quickly turned to the weakness of the State Parliament and the slide toward Bolshevism. I said that I had not at all agreed with Eisner's politics, but the murder committed by Count Arco had brought about much greater confusion than Eisner ever could have. At that point, Frau Joachimsen went into hysterics. "How dare you call the count a murderer!" she screeched, "How dare you blame him for our dire circumstances! He sacrificed himself for us, he roused us, he liberated us from the Galician, I revere him like a savior, I wish I could staunch his wounds, I'm not worthy of unlacing his shoes!" – and she ran out of the room sobbing. Embarrassed and mollifying, her husband explained that his wife was at the end of her tether; her passionate patriotism had taken a terrible blow. I apologized for having upset her, and we parted with a gloomy handshake. Downstairs I declared that we mustn't be swayed in our opinion by these duplicate events, nor draw conclusions about the attitude of the faculty, much less the entire university, based on the crankiness of two hysterical women. Granted, the majority of professors and students may have been a bit more reactionary than democratic, but whenever I got a taste of Hans's Spartacist fanaticism, I could understand the attitude of the academics and, if nothing else, it seemed like the lesser evil. Weckerle was like a demon at Hans's side, enslaving him more and more each day. What I found so exceedingly repellent about Weckerle was the element of impurity about him, the mean slyness mixed with his fanaticism. I view the pure fanatic as an enemy of humanity; he must be rendered harmless, but one can make allowances for his unsoundness of mind and need not hate him. I once asked Weckerle why he was working to promote his idea in Munich, of all places, when he was so proud of his Württemberg mind and so often ridiculed the "Bavarian blockheads." He burst out laughing. "That's precisely why: the dumber, the better – you can get them to do anything." He was not interested in persuading, only in seducing . . . I talked about this repeatedly with Hans, but it didn't help. For him, the blockheads were innocent children who had to be won over to the side of good using childish means – and "good" was embodied by communism, the Spartacus League, the Soviet Republic. Hans had an angel by his side as well, one who was perhaps able to hold him back a tiny bit from the worst entanglements precisely because his robust nature was anything but angelic. This was Hamecher,[154] the sturdy Bavarian who had been a bank officer before the war (during which he had fought on many fronts), and who was now unemployed and forced to earn a living somehow for himself and a war widow, a gentle, quiet woman with whom he lived in informal but close and peaceful companionship. He was a dealer like Hans, and he did not get by entirely without smuggling either. But he set no store by bandit or smuggler romanticism; he maintained a reserve of *bon sens*[155] and uprightness in everything he did, he aspired to be bourgeois once more. When I met him he was in the process of setting himself up as a stamp dealer, and it was through him that I began collecting stamps myself. Just at that time, collecting stamps went from being a pursuit for adolescents and a few adult specialists to a pastime for everyone, and Hamecher revealed to me the interwoven conceptual and practical reasons for this. Now that national borders and forms of government had grown fluid, stamp designs were always changing, so whoever collected them would acquire not only a picture gallery of contemporary history, but also – the word was new to us – something inflation-proof. "If I travel to Zurich with a bundle of hundred-mark notes," Hamecher said to me, "I don't know how many francs they'll give me for them. But if I have a few good stamps in my wallet, then I know where I stand, because their full collector's value will be paid to me in any currency." In later years Hamecher became a respected stamp dealer; the now comfortable and quite legitimate married couple visited us in Dresden, and we chatted about those wild Munich days. But back then, throughout the year 1919, he was not yet able to live solely from dealing in stamps. He once asked my advice regarding the value of a small library that had been consigned to him to be sold and was stacked on the floor of a junk-filled back room in a small attic apartment in Schwabing. I saw in a few glances that he wouldn't get a high price for them. It was the typical book collection of a journalist who'd had more interests than money. Most of the expensive books were paper-bound and stamped "Rez. Ex."[156] and they were in a variety of fields, more often *belles-lettres* and art than history and politics. The books purchased by the owner had, for the most part, been published by Reclam, many of them covering related topics and bound in cheap pasteboard. Philosophical and aesthetic interests were clearly dominant here; there was nothing political to be found. The only foreign-language volume was a schoolbook: *Abrégé de la syntaxe française*.[157] I opened it to find that the cover concealed an anti-militaristic, communist pamphlet printed in Zurich in 1916. All of these books bore a small blue stamp with the name of their owner: Kurt Eisner. It is generally not difficult to determine a person's profession based on their library . . . but without the name marked on the inside, it would have been impossible to guess that this collection of books had belonged to a statesman and prime minister. Eisner's widow had given them to Hans, and Hans had given them to Hamecher. Good angels are seldom capable of doing much to counter evil ones, and Hans would not be dissuaded from joining the Spartacus League. "Hans," I said, "you can't possibly think that this Levien is an honest and decent person." – "Him, honest and decent? He's a panderer, an insane criminal, and I'd say it to his face. But what does that have to do with the essence of the Spartacus League? I've joined precisely because I want to work for the purity of its goals. It is essential to oppose the reactionaries; the government Socialists are even worse than the Junkers before the war, this bloodhound Noske. . ." Hamecher stood by as Hans declaimed like this. "Nothin' you can do about that. . ." he said, smiling. "But listen, Meyerhof, I've been offered a few thousand Swiss cheroots – we could do something with them." – The Council Republic, which had been discussed every day since Eisner's death, ultimately came about suddenly and mysteriously. For the general public in Munich, it started on Monday the 7th of April with a pronouncement from the Central Council[158] and a few proclamations and flyers. The Russian and Hungarian council republics were hailed fraternally, and Weimar – "imperial Germany with republican trappings," as it was described in a proclamation from Erich Mühsam – was renounced. The whereabouts of the Bavarian State Parliament, and the Majority Socialist government under Hoffmann[159] that had been confirmed by it, were unknown at the moment. On this 7th of April and for roughly eight days afterward, the actual ruler of the new Council Republic was, or appeared to be, the People's Deputy for Intellectual Affairs, Gustav Landauer. For me personally, this change involved a particular surprise. A large typewritten note hung on the gate in front of the entrance to the university: the university was closed, the rector, senate, and professors had been dismissed, and after the Easter break a new institution in the service of the people would open with a new faculty. According to Landauer's order, "*per pro.* Strasser." That was my lieutenant from the Spartacus League. But the gate of the now officially closed university was still open a crack, as it had been in the preceding weeks, and there was a great deal of activity. In the hall, a student shouted at a cluster of his colleagues in an agitated, strained voice. I could make out snippets of his sentences: "Those of us from the Works Committee . . . it is on our heads . . . implore you to go home . . . machine guns at any moment . . . danger of a bloodbath . . ." The speech had no effect whatsoever, neither provoking nor intimidating; the students listened with interest, some of them laughing, and did not go home.

The Events at the University of Munich

A.B., Munich, April 8 [1919]

This is a particularly tragicomic chapter. And because it is becoming a matter of growing importance, and because some of it is characteristic and symbolic, so to speak, of the maturity and intellect of the new rulers, I would like to explain in more detail that which I know to be true. I only ask that these facts not be taken as an April Fool's joke. The university here, like the one in Leipzig, I'm sure, had set up so-called preparatory classes. Soldiers who had gone to war without having passed a matriculation exam could take these classes to prepare for the exam while simultaneously starting their university studies. These are, therefore, very young men who are not yet even first-year students, but rather first-year-minus-ones, so to speak. In one of these classes, a lecturer assigned presentation topics about 14 days ago as a practice exercise for the German exam paper. "Herr Strasser, please be prepared to talk about the young Goethe next week." Herr Strasser stands up, 19 years old, in an Austrian uniform without insignia. "Might the Herr Doktor permit me to talk about the Spartacus League and its goals instead of the young Goethe? My fellow students know less about this, and I would like to enlighten them." A flabbergasted lecturer, a fierce rustling of disapproval in the schoolroom – pardon me! the auditorium. To Herr Strasser's credit, it must be said that he eventually accepted the impossibility of his request. But imagine my amazement on Monday when I found a nearly identically worded poster on the closed university: "As the authorized representative of the Central Council, I declare the university to be closed, the senate dismissed, the faculty dissolved. A revolutionary public education institution will open after the break. Strasser." The poster has been overtaken by events, but its essential substance still holds: at this moment, particularly since the resolution that was adopted this morning by all faculties, the university no longer exists. Lectures may still be held until April 12th, and then the farce of the revolutionary institution can begin. Herr Landauer is in charge, and he has six representatives, though it probably suffices to have depicted just one of them. They have formed a revolutionary works committee (!), but they've advised the students to depart and want to bring the new institution into being over Easter.

Of the many assemblies and consultations held on this matter, I want to describe two decisive ones. Yesterday a student assembly convened in the main auditorium, the purpose of which was to clarify and placate. There are 1,000 seats, but twice the number of students crowded in; the windows to the corridors of the top floor had been removed, and whole bundles of academics leaned in through them as well. I have never heard such blustering, such a circus din, such virtuoso shrill whistling, nor such furious, anti-Semitic outbursts. All rage was directed at the small, radical student group that is going along with the new government men. And then came a moment in which something both comical and captivating occurred. Someone read out a manifesto that had been brought in somehow, one which you in Leipzig will certainly have known about for quite some time, but which was entirely new to us in Munich, fed as we are by the truthful socialized press: "The old government still exists, it alone can make changes, it has left Munich and will issue new instructions. Nuremberg, April 7th. Prime Minister Hoffmann." The response was minutes of crazed jubilation, stamping, clapping, shouting, an outburst of enthusiasm the like of which had not been heard here since August 1914. "I had no idea that you students were so socialist-minded," Professor *Schmid Noerr*[160] said afterward. And that was both the comedy and the tragedy of the situation. No, the students here are not at all socialist, and unfortunately the vast majority of them are also not the least bit socially minded nor the least bit politically mature. But they think that, between Hoffmann and Landauer, they are choosing the lesser evil with Hoffmann because, for them, Hoffmann and the old government still embody the nation, order, Fatherland – even if in a sorry state. This jubilation was sad and comical at the same time. Professor Schmid Noerr, who commented ironically on it, was the actual assembly speaker. His task was to develop the reform plans of the socialist student group. He did it in such a way that he was actually able to achieve quiet and calm. Schmid Noerr, from Heidelberg, is a pure idealist. The plans he proposed for a new public education institution (which he intends to publish soon in a book)[161] are fantastically lovely, but unfortunately they also contain some utopian elements and some vaguely banal ones.

But none of this is the primary concern right now. The primary concern became clear today at a critical meeting of the entire faculty under the chairmanship of the prorector, *von Müller* (the renowned physician). "They want to see scalps," said a professor who had negotiated with Landauer. "The internal, actual academic changes are much less important to them." In short: they cannot conjure up their new public education institution out of thin air, they need part of the old teaching staff. But only the part that is politically acceptable to them – they want the other part to disappear. Including Max von Weber,[162] for example – he's not "liberal" enough for them. To counter this, it was unanimously agreed today that if one person is relieved, everyone will go for the sake of academic freedom – that is, they will stop lecturing. They will not resign from office, because they have declared that the new ruling powers have no authority to take it from them.

Even after this, the university did not actually close. The dismissed senate continued to hold office, the dismissed professors still gave a few sparsely attended lectures before the imminent break,[163] and several stormy meetings took place in the main auditorium and smaller assembly hall, without the threatened machine guns ever making an appearance. Only a single evening lecture about the Communist Manifesto was held by a non-academic party member. The main auditorium was tightly packed, by no means just with students, but also definitely not with proletarians. I saw nothing but intelligentsia, a lot of Schwabing,[164] a lot of the decidedly middle-class – on the whole, the usual audience for a popular academic lecture. And the lecture by Comrade Otto Thomas was also no different than any of the dozens of popular lectures that had been held at public education institutions under the old regime. It was no more profound, no more lacking in foreign words, it was not provocative. But the Council Republic ensured a grandiose prelude. Prior to the speaker, a student from the revolutionary university council stepped up to the lectern and shouted: "Comrades! Compatriots! I bid you welcome – today still as half-guests, but from tomorrow as the owners of this building and this entire institution. The bourgeoisie is supported by three pillars: militarism, bureaucracy and the educational monopoly of the property owners. Today we are shattering the third pillar." Strasser – I did not see him again, and in recent years I've wondered futilely whether there might have been some connection between him and the protagonists of the same name in the Nazi Party[165] – Strasser tried in vain to assert his will by locking a few file cabinets belonging to the refractory senate and taking the keys. This scene had an amusing postlude. The day after Munich was occupied by Reich troops, a young girl visited Prorector Müller,[166] the same physician to whom I had given my oath of office in 1914,[167] and who was now representing Rector Baeumker in a very calm and dignified way. (Baeumker, who had briefly been arrested as a hostage, did not feel up to dealing with the commotion and had reported in sick.) In tears, the girl explained that she was supposed to deliver the senate keys; she had gotten them from her older sister, who had been given them by a friend, who in turn had been friends with the sister of the vanished Strasser. The little girl had gotten scared along the way and thrown the keys into the Isar River – and then she had gotten truly scared and now wanted to confess everything.

The Third Revolution in Bavaria

(From our A.B. correspondent)

Munich, April 9 [1919]
Rumors. – The indifference of the bourgeoisie. – Dr. Quidde. – The men of the day. – Levien, Landauer, Epp. – No "Leipzig-style" general strike. – "Prussian and Jew." – The plane.

By the time this dispatch reaches you – phone calls and telegraphs "abroad" are being monitored, the threat of the revolutionary tribunal is reiterated on every street corner and in every possible context, and the reason I have little desire to wear the martyr's crown for the Bavarian bourgeoisie will become clear from my account – so by the time you receive my dispatch, we may already be on our fourth or fifth partner here. My report has no major news to offer from Munich, but it can relate a few things to make the heroically epic seem a little bit more human.

Anyone who has experienced the fine equanimity of *Munich's bourgeoisie* will not be overly surprised by the successful coup de main of the council party. The bourgeoisie and all of the moderates were not unsuspecting this time; there had been whispers everywhere for weeks, and then in April "it" happened. But the good burghers decided that they had been politically agitated for long enough, and at some point a man had to have "his peace." So they concerned themselves with butter and eggs instead of Mühsam and Landauer. The soviet people were more sensible, they combined business with – business: namely, foraging trips with educational speeches in the countryside. I know about these propaganda trips; they've been at work out there, and in Munich's military barracks as well. Now the Munich garrison marches through the city with red flags to demonstrate for the Council Republic, and the third revolution can boast of having triumphed literally without firing a single shot or spilling a drop of blood. So far, at least – because the majority is gradually realizing that it has just been ambushed.

Such a characteristic scene last Friday evening. A Democratic assembly. Dr. *Quidde*,[168] the Democrat and parliamentarian for Weimar, was supposed to talk about Bavarian foreign policy, while a local member of the State Parliament would talk about Bavarian domestic policy. The assembly was very well attended by bourgeois standards; probably half a thousand attentive and pleasantly quiet and peaceful listeners (even their interjections were peaceful), sitting with beers.

The local delegate who was meant to talk about Munich politics was "unfortunately indisposed with hoarseness," but Dr. Quidde – tall, refined, balding, graying, with a sharp little beard and sharp (prototypically Bavarian!) enunciation, you could hear the *s*-alient points and elegant thought *ex*-periments – kept us most entertained. There was a "provisional statement of accounts from Weimar," which became a hymn of praise to Weimar, where there was actually much less talk and much more action, where they had given the Reich a leadership and an emergency constitution, where they had cautiously begun to nationalize. Cautiously, and if Bavaria, with its devastated economic life, preferred to move at a different pace – "then we'll wait!" And that is just what we did, we waited.

Meanwhile, as the final knot was being tied in the council net outside, Dr. Quidde grew inflamed with patriotic passion. He spoke of our German hardship in the East, which was also Bavaria's hardship, and he championed the Freikorps. But the fact that all recruitment is forbidden here under penalty of severe punishment, that recruitment appeals are only making their way in from the north in pathetic secrecy and cannot be disseminated – this was mentioned only with the feeblest protest. On this account, it was necessary to massage the special feelings of the Bavarians all the more emphatically and zealously. Because one certainly could, and certainly would, get the impression that those in the East were serving the Prussians. No, not that, absolutely not! And then he really warmed up, for then he came to Bavaria's special position, to its territorial privileges, and as a Democrat he obviously could not stand up for these territorial privileges – only for the Bavarian safeguards. This had to be made palatable, and this was also the only point at which the placid audience was roused enough to shout interjections and questions. You all want your own Bavarian Minister of War? For God's sake, no! Then Prussia will appoint its own Minister of War again, and he'll rule us now just as he reigned over us before. People shout that Berlin still reigned in every respect anyway. Dr. Quidde grows scornful. "Are you still afraid of Berlin?" A shout: "The head-count is in its favor!" With a flash of genius, the grinning speaker retorts: "Headcount? If only we had those heads!" Oh, we have them in abundance, nothing but true Bavarian heads quite over-flowing with political wisdom: Landauer, Mühsam, Levien, Lipp,[169] Toller,[170] Neurath[171] und Wadler[172] ... I could continue the Homeric list and eventually come to Dr. Quidde's name.

Quidde's speech ended with a request for a *protest resolution* against the dictated peace. This was accepted, and then the debat-ers followed. Against Berlin and Prussia, of course. This always unites them, the ones from the Right and the Left and the Center. And then the joke of the evening: one of them declares, "Why are we still quarreling about Weimar and the current republic? At this point it's practically a thing of the past!" And fellow party members shout at the man that he shouldn't tell tales out of school. Then everyone goes home feeling reassured after having done their civic duty, and they read in the newspaper that "the most serious events" are imminent, and they hear that

the Council Republic was already openly announced during an assembly held at the same time, and that the *State Parliament* is no longer allowed to meet! And then they go to bed. And on Saturday, in a state of utter equa-nimity, they hear that the Central Council is convening, and that the *Council Republic* will certainly be proclaimed, and that this is just the way it is and they have to accept it. No outward disturbance whatsoever, not the slightest hint of resistance. The strangest thing is that, this time, absolutely no names are mentioned, either from the old government or the new one to come. The old one has disappeared for Munich – the new one is nameless, shrouded in darkness. There is a Central Council, and most people know nothing more than that. Only on Sunday and Monday did the veil lift somewhat. It was then we heard with astonishment that things had been very "moderate" in the Central Council.

Oh yes, the lovely mani-festo that connects us with our Russian and Hungarian brothers and separates us from Weimar, from "imperial Germany with republican trappings" as Mühsam put it so handsomely in a decree today, is a modest declaration. In the decisive meeting, *Levien* called for an *immediate declaration of war* against this very same "imperial Germany" but met with no success. For the time being, at least. This is good to know for future developments, because now that opposition is gradually beginning to stir, the new government – with its Red Army, its Revolutionary Tribunal and its good intentions – will, in all likelihood, shift even further to the left if they have to fight first. I do not want to prophesize, but I believe that the man to come is *Levien*, the current one is *Landauer*, and the next but one is *Epp*.[173] I described Levien in an earlier dispatch; Landauer, who is currently the People's Deputy for Public Enlightenment and probably the actual intellectual leader of the new government, appears to me to be Eisner reincarnate, not one bit smarter, but a good bit more radical. An idealist like him, a poet like him, a bohemian like him, miles removed from all political necessities and certainties like him (just a few miles more

removed), with fingers as free of blood and money as Eisner's fingers, and surely, just like Eisner, soon to be forced into acts of violence or forced aside by the violence of others. Epp: a colonial officer and daredevil in 1904, then the first bourgeois in the Lifeguards regiment,[174] a *colonel* and leader of the Lifeguards since December 1914, severely feared and yet loved by the troops, leading them in Verdun and the fiercest assaults elsewhere, and now the almost enigmatic recruiter of a "Noske Freikorps" on the Bavarian border. Is it really just a "Noske corps," will it really only be used against the East, is it really still outside of Bavaria? As of yesterday, we here know that the old government still exists – but its location is still a mystery to us in Munich, and the "Austria is united in your camp"[175] does not entirely silence the posters on the street warning of the severest punishment for "nonsensical rumors."

Looking back, I wonder when the all-too-still bourgeois waters first showed evidence of the ripples that hint at a coming flood. It was so miserable, so pathetic on

Saturday and Sunday and even Monday, in the first hours after the proclamation of the Council Republic[176] and the "national holiday," the way all of this was accepted with dull bafflement and more leisure than dignity. The way it was declared at an academic assembly that a *Leipzig-style general strike* was out of the question, as there was no consensus among the civil servants, and 30 percent of the doctors would not go along with it. But the Central Council played at being Xerxes and whipped the sluggish sea. The *closure of the banks* was a joke too far for many; they had to be reopened today, and reassuring explanations – coupled with threats, of course – had to be offered.

But what good is the most reassuring explanation if I am not allowed to withdraw more than 100 marks a day? And when my newspaper announces the imminent expropriation of homes? And illustrates this with lovely woodcuts depicting – almost futuristically – the misery and "salvation" of the proletariat? The newspaper has to resort to such pictures just to halfway fill its sparse pages, because other than Spartacist editorials, all it has available to it are decrees from the Central Council. It has nothing else, literally nothing else, to print any more. Germany and the world no longer exist – there is only the Soviet Republic of Munich. Incidentally, the local *Neueste Nachrichten* isn't playing along here any more, so the press department of the Central Council is publishing the paper itself.

So the agitation – which, I should say in advance, is still in a stage of torpor, still generally a calm before the storm – gradually swelled. It expressed itself neither beautifully nor cleverly, but *anti-Semitically*. And it thus gave the tyrannical government the opportunity to make liberal gestures; the posters from the Central Council warn against the *persecution of Jews*. In truth, the Jews have it no better than the Prussians here; they share the fate of being blamed for everything, and depending on the situation they are either the capitalists or the Bolshevists. I think if you asked a real Spartacist whether Noske was a Prussian or a Jew, he'd reply: "Both." And if you asked the petite bourgeoisie of Munich whether Levien was a Jew or a Prussian, you'd get the same answer: "Both." And in both cases the answer would be wrong. . . . An automobile stopped on the Odeonplatz, and its occupants read out and distributed flyers about the dictatorship of the proletariat. Immediately there was a bellowing chorus of "Jews! Jewish pigs!" But a squad of soldiers approached, a mixture of infantrymen and sailors, shouldering rifles and even light machine guns. Everyone scattered, some taking cover in the lobbies of apartment buildings to watch and wait . . . Students clamored before the closed university, anti-Semitic enough in their own right. A fellow student from the "Works Council" implored them to disperse because there might be machine guns here soon, because "the Revolutionary Tribunal could have our heads." They went – but nasty anti-Semitic flyers appeared.

As I bring this report to a close in the hopes of taking it to the evening train, a *plane* is pouring its messages out of a blue sky. From Nuremberg or somewhere else? From Hoffman, from Epp? I do not need to wait until the children downstairs have tracked down the news. Out in Leipzig, they've already long known what remains hidden from us. . . .

Revolutionary Diary

Munich, April 17, 1919

No longer a dispatch, now just a diary, undertaken in total, threefold seclusion. Threefold, because outside the "White Guards" are holding Munich to siege, and inside a tenth of the population at most, and I mean at the very most (Munich is not an industrial city, after all!), is holding the remaining hundreds of thousands as if in chains, and this tenth, in turn, the "Red Guard" and class-conscious proletariat, is the utterly will-less and oblivious tool of a tiny handful of foreign adventurers who feud with one another and whose visionary and bohemian natures must of necessity give way to more robust criminal characters hour by hour. This is entirely unexaggerated. Total obliviousness is the mental state seen again and again in every social class and party. Munich passively accepts its tragicomic fate, and even the apparently dominant proletariat is quite passive, allowing itself to be pushed hither and thither. Passivity is the only truly Bavarian ingredient in this revolution, one which is feigned by non-Bavarians and childishly copied by foreign names and foreign institutions.

The first part of my simple prophecy – "Landauer followed by Levien, Levien followed by Epp" – was fulfilled on Sunday, after this distressing middle section of events was nearly avoided (if only the citizens of Munich had had

marrow in their bones instead of some beer-like liquid) thanks to the fortitude of a small crowd in the city. It came to pass that the Council Republic felt insecure, mistrusted by the bourgeoisie on the Right, harried by the communists on the Left, who had only "derision and scorn for the monstrosity of the Council Republic" (this is according to the "Notices from the Executive Council of the Workers' and Soldiers' Councils" from April 16th; the paper is distributed free of charge and is our only newspaper). The growing insecurity of the ruling powers was reflected in the vast number of flyers that they tossed out of cars onto the streets, that they distributed and pasted everywhere. Invocations of unity within the proletariat, announcements that this unity had been achieved now that communist representatives had been included in the Central Council, and, above all, recruitment flyers, always recruitment flyers for the Red Army. One of these flyers reads: "According to reliable sources, Noske threatened to march to Bavaria with his infamous paid assassins ... Even in Munich, the reactionaries are on the march, and their most qualified blossoms, the students, have already sentenced the honest representatives of the proletariat to death . . . For this reason, comrades and compatriots, report in masses to the Red Army!" But the masses have failed to appear for the time being, even though the pay is very good. A Red Guard now gets 19 marks a day; for this, even the current "honest representatives of the proletariat" have allowed the bourgeois bank safes to be opened. But I am getting ahead of myself with the inroads (and setbacks) of our nameless leaders; I'm still on the "old" government, the Central Council. At noon on Sunday, all of Munich was amazed. The regiments, individually and by name, had just rallied behind the Central Council, most idealistically seeing as they were still receiving not 19 marks but, even as enlisted Red Guards, "only" 14 – and suddenly there was a poster, laconically and mysteriously signed by "The Munich Garrison," declaring that the Central Council had been demolished, the garrison was "discussing" its statement on the Hoffmann government, and food trains were standing at the ready for Munich. Amazement all around. No one knew what had happened, but everyone could see that the "power" of the government, of the ever-so-popular Central Council, had been shattered somehow. And what conclusions does the citizen of Munich draw from something like this? – Who would draw conclusions on a holy Sunday in Munich? That would be Prussian hustle-bustle! But in the evening, as everyone peacefully strolled around the triumphal arch at Siegestor, a clatter arose in the city center. First gunshots, then increasingly protracted streaks of machine-gun fire, then a hefty combination of the two melodies mixed with a few hand grenades, and then, after about an hour, three mighty, echoing booms and, immediately afterward, what the French would inevitably call *un silence tragique*,[177] but what the residents of Munich simply embraced as a welcome end to the nocturnal disturbance of the peace. We then slept blissfully and awoke on Monday under the protection of Levien, who, without actually stepping forward to be named, now in fact rules Munich as the leader of the local Spartacists. "Proletarians! Soldiers! Fighters! Victory! Victory! Victory! The train station has been stormed! . . . The first day of the glorious battle of Munich's class-conscious proletariat! . . . Bring on the Noskes, the Epps, the Schneppenhorsts![178] We'll give them a reception!" This was how a communist flyer rejoiced with interminable bombast. But it honestly had not been a glorious battle. Those who had rebelled against Munich's Russian republic had been a small heap of a Republican Protection Force led by the notably hated train station commander Aschenbrenner.[179] In their naïve, sunny optimism, they had probably counted on support from more level-headed circles. But they were left alone, and they succumbed to superior numbers and their mortars. And now, of course, Levien's hour had come. The communists had stormed the train station and saved the noble Russian-Bavarian state; they then thrust aside the limp Central Council government and established the long-awaited total dictatorship of the proletariat.

The replacement newspaper of April 16th that was mentioned earlier also included a bold-print statement from Landauer: "I acknowledge and welcome the restructuring. The old Central Council no longer exists, and I offer my strength to the Action Committee to be used wherever it is needed." But this strength cannot be used yet, because it is moderated.

One thing you do have to admire about the new government: it has given the city a thoroughly martial air, it knows how to "impress" the population – indeed, it knows how to inject bright new colors into the almost boring uniformity of the revolutionary scene that has dominated so many German cities for months, helping it regain its somewhat drunkenly shaky footing. It should go without saying that there are strikes. But we also have public notices ordering citizens to turn in their weapons within 12 hours "under penalty of death." And we have an ever-growing number of armed civilians; class-conscious, their shotguns on their back – occasionally even female. And the military! Infantrymen and sailors march together – or, more precisely, stroll in a jumble. Rifles, the muzzles pointing down, hang coquettishly loose from straps; field-gray scarves are worn around the neck and dangle to the belt, with cartridge clips stuck in them; three or four long-handled hand grenades are worn on the belt, wide red bands are worn around the arm. It looks more like the Wild West than Munich – and yet it does still look like Munich: Texas as designed by Gulbransson.[180] At three in the afternoon, the government reports directly to the people. On the balcony of the Wittelsbach Palace, the fortress-like red English castle where, in early August 1914, King Ludwig stood surrounded by his staff and addressed the cheering volunteers beneath the tall trees of the forecourt, there now stands the Berlin communist Werner, preaching to his followers who have taken the place of the volunteers of 1914: "Comrades, compatriots! You can trust in our cause. Comrade Levien is working for all of you in the Ministry of War, and Comrade Toller beseeched to be given the most dangerous post:

he is at the front!" The "front," which defies the White Guards and is said (we already have proper war reports) to have won a great victory yesterday, is thought to be in the direction of Dachau, and a special Munich army camp fills the cordoned-off Hofgarten. The headquarters is there, too, in the Army Museum, where City Commandant Egelhofer[181] is based. They say (I cannot verify it but believe it to be very likely) that he did his preparatory studies with the sailors in Kiel. We have had to do without the emotion of actual combat activity since last Sunday, now that the front has advanced so far, as the few bangs from anxious or cheerful sentries have become part of the usual sounds of the city, just as the racket of the electric trains once was in strike-free times. But for this, too, the resourceful government has found an original substitute: it rings the church bells incessantly whenever anything stirs outside the city. This was the case the evening before last; theatrical performances were even cut off mid-act. And yesterday the incessant ringing was reprised very romantically around midnight; in the moment of surprise it was tempting to shout "Happy New Year!" The war game continues by day, too, and is by no means limited to hackneyed, red-flagged military jaunts. A Bamberg government plane appears, circling low, and is immediately surrounded by a rattle of infantry fire for having approached the Türkenkaserne; the Lifeguards inside had initially wanted to remain neutral – but who can remain neutral on a wage of 19 marks? However, the new government is not only martial, it is also concerned with feeding and educating the people. I already mentioned that it is opening the bank safes, but it is also opening the larders of the hotels, boarding schools, and bourgeois populace. Patrols search everywhere for food, as it is of prime importance to ensure the sustenance of the "working" classes. And the *nutrimentum spiritus*[182] is catered for by this notice from my young friend Strasser: the university, previously the property of a privileged class, now belongs to the people. On Thursday evening, Comrade Thomas will begin a series of lectures in the main auditorium on the topic of communism. I wonder whether they'll let me in? – When it comes to newspapers, however, we are in a very bad way. Whether it's worse than under the Central Council, however, I don't know. Now we are just handed that news bulletin, whereas before we believed we were reading a proper newspaper, although apart from the decrees of the Council Republic we were only reading essays by Voltaire, Stirner, Marx and Hölderlin (!) – but not untalented Bolshevist journalists, mind you. And we could admire the futuristic woodcuts as well. In the final days of Landauer's glory, a delegation of typesetters from the *Münchener Neueste* newspaper visited him. They asked him not to take the bread from their mouths by suppressing the publisher. Landauer replied that the Council Republic would never take the bread from any worker's mouth – on the contrary! So they made a request: could he please, for the love of God, at least stop publishing the awful "little pictures"? He then gave them a lecture about revolutionary arts. The total suppression of all news naturally leads to rumors upon rumors. When shots were fired at the plane yesterday, it was immediately said that the plane had been shot down, and a few hours later it was said that Hoffmann himself, the prime minister, had been in the plane and was now dead as a doornail. And the things they say about the "front"! One moment there are precisely 120,000 White Guards in Dachau, and Epp is already in Nymphenburg, and tonight (it's always "tonight") he is going to pummel Munich with heavy artillery, and the next moment the "Whites" have been routed by the Red Army near Allach and have run away pathetically. . .

Among all of these changing impressions and reports, which fit like a dream with the current splendid April weather, only one thing remains absolutely constant: the stoic calm with which Munich's bourgeois husband and wife sit in the window for hours, as motionless as if they were part of the building's architecture. Time and again, the real Munich sits and watches the revolutionary games of foolish foreign figures. And admittedly, it can now do nothing more than watch – it is completely helpless. And if no salvation comes from the outside, then all conviviality will ultimately end and the comical aspect of the Munich tragicomedy will shrivel to nothing. Even then, a proper tragedy will probably not come of all this, because for that to happen, grandeur and dignity would have to belong to the victors and the defeated alike. –

April 18, 1919

Yesterday afternoon I met Gustav Landauer, who for a few days held the fate, and specifically the intellectual fate, of Munich – though he himself hoped it was Bavaria – in his hands. Only the long-hanging hair gave him away as an oddity; in other respects, the gaunt man with the full graying beard makes an entirely cultivated impression, neither revolutionary nor proletarian; the look in his large brown eyes is much more benevolent than fanatic, and there is a polished mildness to his voice and manner of expression. "If you want to know the future of the university (he says somewhat gloomily), you'll have to ask Herr Hoffmann. Things won't continue like this for very much longer. And I can't decree anything; Herr Levien has to sign everything. These people take a purely materialistic view of their republic, and for all that, they have only the smallest city republic – the entire state is against them ... I, on the other hand, wanted to work on the intellect." I take him at his word, and yet I cannot feel sorry for him. Anyone who could be pushed aside so quickly by the worst elements has proven his political incompetence. But this is the farthest thing from intellectual incompetence. "I would definitely have reformed the university during the three-week break," Landauer said. Whether it would have benefited from this reform? It's very doubtful. He wanted to shunt off the academics incapable of teaching, he wanted to give financial security to the lecturers, he wanted to make the classes more lively – but when it came to economics and history classes during the "transition periods," he wanted to exclusively bring in

socialists who would promulgate the "truth" about how Prussia and Bavaria had both been "stolen," and who would not set themselves up as defenders of capitalism like the "arch-reactionary" Max Weber. Because I smiled at him a bit when he mentioned the word "truth," he immediately added that even he was aware of the relativity of this concept, but he insisted that now was the time to speak aloud, single-handedly and very loudly, that which had previously been kept silent. And as for the faculty of law, if it was just training civil servants, he would have scrapped it altogether! After all, he had even told the top officials in his Ministry of Culture that they now had to "forget their legal spirit." No, I cannot regret that he so quickly played out his role as an autocrat. He is a motivator, a journalist, a great but very childish talent. And even the most talented child will do damage when he high-handedly toys with adult things. Thus it was that, for all of the intellectualization, this fine journalist even damaged the press for as long as he was in charge of it. "I'm going to turn my newspaper into a book," he says proudly and, in doing so, passes judgment on it himself – because there is a difference between a collection of essays and a newspaper. He is a child, and I hope for his sake (and the sake of us all) that no one makes a martyr of him . . .

I also asked Landauer who Comrade Otto Thomas was, the man who was supposed to talk about the Communist Manifesto at the university that evening. "A trade-union secretary who has just discovered his communist heart, who has one foot in present-day Munich and the other in Bamberg." At seven I went to the main auditorium. At least 1,500 people were packed into it. Who I did not see, however, were the workers. Nothing but intelligentsia. A lot of Schwabing (Café Stefanie must have been empty), a lot of the decidedly middle-class, on the whole the usual audience for popular academic lectures. And it was the usual lecture – which would just as likely have been heard an average of dozens of times at public education institutions and similar establishments under the *ancien régime* – that was now dutifully recited to patient ears. It was lacking all excitement, all sen-

sation, all innovation. But there was a reason for the whole scene, of course. Prior to the speaker, a student from the revolutionary university council stepped up to the podium: "Compatriots, comrades! I bid you welcome, today still as half-guests, but from tomorrow as the owners of this building, this entire institution. The bourgeoisie was supported by three pillars: by militarism, by bureaucracy, and by the educational monopoly of the property owners. Today we are shattering the third pillar!" It sounded wonderful, but it stood in rather humorous contrast to what actually happened.

But let's not be too particular in this regard. After all, we're bringing down "militarism" by imitating it so exquisitely. The general staff reports from the front are increasingly Ludendorff-ish in style. "Rosenheim is firmly in our grasp" – "Dachau taken. Our troops, who fought exceedingly well, pushed beyond it. Several hundred prisoners, four cannons . . . (etc. etc.) remained in our hands." All that's missing is the old "Bring out the flags!" For now they're making due with "Bring out the food!" instead, though the humor is finally in danger of being drowned in wretchedness. A poster appeared today warning the control commissions that they must actually hand over any hoarded goods they confiscate, so the Council Republic can distribute them fairly to "the sick, the elderly, and combatants." There certainly won't be much more to distribute under this government, since even the greatest optimists calculate that Munich's food supplies will only last for another fourteen days at most. Munitions, on the other hand, we apparently have in abundance; the amount of ammunition fired two different times yesterday at planes from Bamberg would have been enough to hold off a small assault in Flanders.

A.B.

Ridiculousness was one of the main characteristics I associated with the Council Republic, such abject and utter ridiculousness that for the longest time I thought it was highly unlikely the pathetic affair would come to a truly bloody end. There would probably be a few victims, because scuffles were part of the fun, after all – but actual streams of blood flowing as in a proper battle? Nonsense! It was all just a farce. Was the famous Gustav Landauer a less ridiculous figure than the anonymous Strasser? In February, when Eisner was still alive but not yet a leading statesman, merely a respected writer, I had seen and heard him speak in the Odeon concert hall at the memorial for Karl Liebknecht.[183] The slight man in a black coat with the black, flowing mane of a prophet had spoken in the lyrical tones of a prophet about the successor to Luther – to whom Liebknecht traced back his genealogy – who had wanted to bring peace to the world as an earthly savior, and who had died as a martyr. Landauer had referred to himself as a "non-political politician" at the time, and also as a devotee of the true republic, the Council Republic, and an enemy of the Weimar lie. Now I was able to meet him in person. Weckerle was his secretary, and they sat together at Hans Meyerhof's, where he seemed to feel comfortable, more comfortable than in the Ministry of Culture, whose councilors and secretaries irritated him. He had announced that he wanted to do

away with bureaucracy, he wanted to put everything in order himself –
whereupon an entire day's worth of mail had been placed in a laundry
basket on his desk: a secondary school wanted permission to hold a
sports day for its upper classes, the gymnasium of a girls' school was in
need of repair, a preparatory school was looking for a replacement for
its deceased caretaker, et cetera, et cetera. He had asked how his predecessor had dealt with this heap of trifling matters. Well, the gentlemen
from the individual departments would have done the groundwork
for the minister so that he would not be burdened by trivialities. Then
things should perhaps stay as they were for the time being, Landauer
had decided. When I first met him at Hans's, he was still a minister
but had already surpassed the extent of his literally ephemeral power.
In private conversation, he lost some of the aura of a prophet. His long
hair was certainly eccentric, and even now there was a slightly lyrical
note to his voice, but he spoke in a thoroughly unaffected manner, and
the look in his brown eyes was more benevolent than regal or fanatic.
My impression was that he was somewhat more than Eisner in every
respect: somewhat more serious, somewhat more educated, somewhat
more idealistic, somewhat more radical (without any bloodlust), and
somewhat more ill-suited to being a statesman. "In three weeks," he
said, "I would have reformed the university – it lies closest to my heart
and is also the most important matter –, but I can no longer decree
anything without Levien's countersignature." – "How would you
have done it yourself?" He warmed up and elaborated, yet remained
comfortably abstract on the most critical points. He would have made
it easier to be admitted to the university, he would have forced the
professors to teach in a more naturalistic way, he would have dismissed
those who were very behind the times, he would have scrapped the
faculty of law if it existed solely to train civil servants, and he would
have insisted on academic freedom – historians would have had to be
able to explain, openly and without false glorification, how Prussia
had been stolen. I asked him what he wanted to do about freedom of
teaching in the economics department. He said an exception would
have to be made there, but only for a transitional period, only for

the education and rectification of a generation. Socialist teaching had been muzzled for all too long at the university, and now only socialists should hold professorships in economics. I had heard the story about the incoming mail in the laundry basket from Vossler, who had been regaled by a ministry official who was not at all prone to telling tales, and at the time I had thought it was a joke, or at least an exaggeration; now I believed every word of it. I met with Landauer once more, three days before the end of what I still believed to be a comedy. He had resigned from his post,[184] as he did not want to share any of the blame for the havoc wreaked by Levien. He himself had aspired to an ideal council republic in Bavaria and in Germany, he said, but Levien was turning it into a Munich prison. Hans Meyerhof laughed – for all of his enthusiasm, the whole thing was just a splendid game to him – and he showed off the identification card he had just received from the office of the Spartacus League: "Party Comrade Hans Meyerhof is authorized to arrest counter-revolutionary individuals." I asked him how he had come by this card. He said it had been forced on him; if I wanted, he could get one for me, too – things were fairly wild there at the moment. "Use your authority," Landauer said, "and arrest Levien." Those were the last words I heard from the poor Don Quixote: he was bludgeoned to death by peasants as he attempted to escape.[185]

There were cruder absurdities in the Council Republic than Landauer's fine tragicomedy. The most representative expression of the new state were the two institutions which, through their resonant names, linked the state to the Russian Council Republic and the great French Revolution: namely, the Red Army and the Revolutionary Tribunal. Parts of the Red Army – when they weren't standing on trucks and driving through the streets with their rifles at the ready – constantly trotted around (you couldn't really say marched) in mixed squads, soldiers and sailors jumbled together. The red armbands, the caps worn askew and the rifles hanging downward from their straps were familiar to me from Wilna and Leipzig. But the Munich revolutionaries were much more picturesque. Wide, field-gray scarves with cartridge clips stuck in them dangled to their belts, which were studded

with three to four long-handled hand grenades. Each squad also had
not a few soldiers carrying their rifles with the muzzle pointing up so
they could display a plume of feathers. These feathers now took the
place of the sprays of flowers from the summer of 1914; they came
from the pheasants that were bred in the English Garden. The Red
military hunted there, sometimes with infantry rifles, sometimes with
light machine guns. This diversion was not entirely harmless, because
when their comrades in the city heard the clatter from the English
Garden, they were occasionally deceived into thinking there was actual
danger, and they fired warning shots in return. Once a day shots were
fired all over the city, for a different reason, but clearly with just as
much delight as during a pheasant hunt. A plane would appear regularly in the late afternoon and scatter flyers. In these flyers, Hoffmann's
legitimate government, which had fled to Bamberg, encouraged the
people of Munich to take heart: their liberators were on the way. Anti-
aircraft guns were stationed in the Hofgarten, and to back them up,
rifle shots were fired from the streets, out of windows and from the
roofs of the houses and barracks; laughter and shouts mixed with the
bangs, it was great fun. Nothing ever happened to the plane, and this
scene became as much a part of the expected daily routine as the sunset.
At first Hans said to me: "No liberators will come, they don't dare send
Bavarian troops to march on Munich, and as for Prussians – if you're
not Bavarian, you're a Prussian! – they certainly don't dare send them.
And who would be liberated? The bourgeoisie is quiet, and nothing
will happen to them if they stay quiet. Your students should watch out,
though." But then – no one knew the specifics, as all of the newspapers,
with the exception of the news bulletin from the Munich government,
had been suppressed, and postal service had been interrupted – then
troops were apparently on the march after all. The recruitment notices
for the Red Army took on a pleading, imploring tone; posters threatened the reactionaries in Munich with death; besides soldiers you saw
armed civilians with red armbands, most of them workers from the
Maffei machine factory; and from time to time church bells would ring
and factory sirens would wail to raise the alarm. And then came victory

reports from the front, which was supposed to be near Dachau, victory reports which, in their imitation of the army telegrams about the great battles of the world war, sounded comical again. No, I did not take this whole affair seriously, it was a springtime carnival commotion, it was a masquerade, it was a scuffle at most. And the bourgeois hostages who had been decently housed in a hotel would remain unharmed as well. They were just playing at revolution. I took the behavior of the Revolutionary Tribunal to be a kind of proof that the hostages were safe. You cannot hear those words without seeing the glinting machete before your eyes and smelling the dripping blood. And how fitting it was that along with the many posters warning of the death penalty, there was now an actual Revolutionary Tribunal sitting in the old Palace of Justice. I attended a session.[186] [. . .]

April 19, 1919

"Revolutionary Tribunal" in the Palace of Justice. With the lavish rococo decoration of its ornate staircase, the Palace of Justice fits splendidly with tableaux from 1792, the age of Danton; I would bet that the artistic directors of our Munich revolution very much took this into consideration. Landauer is an expert, after all, as demonstrated by his letters from the French Revolution.[187] At the Stachus entrance, a few sailors demand to see my identification. As it is fatally bourgeois in nature, my bags are very politely patted down for weapons. Then I am allowed to pass, without having to relinquish my penknife, which I showed them. Up in the corridors there is much coming and going. A courtroom for the regional court bears a large new inscription: "Courtroom of the Revolutionary Tribunal," while a room next to it has been designated as a "Reception Room for the Revolutionary Tribunal," and in general this significant phrase is repeated readily and often. Workers with shotguns and red sashes slung over their shoulders, and soldiers with hand grenades, stand around in fairly large numbers. The courtroom looks no different than it did under the old regime; some prince in a general's uniform still hangs undisturbed above the judges' platform. I have to wait a rather long time for the entrance of the tribunal that is in "permanent" session. And this is not the least bit boring, because in the gallery – where uniformed and civilian "compatriots and comrades" sit smoking and armed, and where the female element is also present and accounted for – the most animated conversation is under way. A tall worker toying with a shotgun has just returned from the front and is recounting the great victory at Dachau: how the Whites ran away, how they "all" wore 1st Class Iron Crosses, which were taken from the prisoners, how the victors received a bonus of two pounds of smoked meat. Another relates that only workers are allowed to use the railroad now, "not the better folk" – "but they all wanna be workers now, intellectual workers." The contempt he pours into the word "intellectual" is indescribable, and honestly, he is right to be contemptuous. How much opportunism and foppery have taken hold here. Schwabing is playing at world revolution – it would

be enough to make you laugh if it weren't also enough to make you despair, because the growing obstinacy of the actual proletarians is no game. Someone brought up the latest proposal, that the "capitalists" – who "are different people than us" – should be checkmated once and for all. "In every house where twelve bourgeois live, we immediately lodge twenty proletarians. Then they can't budge, and if the Whites do show up, we shoot from every window." Afterward, the question of moral reformation is seriously addressed. "Prostitution" will no longer exist since the bourgeoisie alone is to blame for it. They know they all have to marry for money, so they want to make love beforehand and seduce the daughters of the people!! This is stated with conviction and receives lively applause. Finally the tribunal appears. A gray-haired woman and four men serving as judges, two men serving as the "speaker" (heretofore prosecutor) and the recorder. I would almost have said one lady and four gentleman, because there is nothing proletarian and certainly nothing bloodthirsty about them; in fact, they look staidly middle-class and almost incongruously benevolent, as if they wanted to reassuringly indicate that they were not lions but only Snug the Joiner.[188] (No one has yet been sentenced to death – at most to a few months in prison, as I hear someone whisper behind me.) A heavily armed man then leads in the criminal: a lanky, boyish fellow with a wild head of hair, wearing shabby field-gray. Two witnesses appear at the same time. "I'm Frank Ludwig's lover and I ain't swearin'," the younger woman immediately declares. "Now gimme your hand and promise to tell the truth – like you've taken an oath," the chairman says. Then, always half in dialect, he very briefly reads out the facts of the case and conducts a short, intense interrogation. Frank Ludwig was nabbed in the Soller, a tavern apparently notorious for such dealings, after buying 100 meat ration stamps for 145 marks and trying to sell them again for 200 marks. "Didn't you think to yourself that you were hurting the poor by doing that?" – "Nah!" There isn't much more to get out of this "offender against the revolution." He just keeps repeating that he's a peddler in the country-side and couldn't get home 'cause no trains were running and he had to make a living, after all. And that he's war-disabled, three seizures a week – his lover and landlady could back him up. After a few minutes, the "speaker" is given the floor. "The man must be punished" is all he says. The chairman stands up, but the man next to him tugs on his coat. He sits down again. "Alright then, the defense!" A gentleman rises behind the accused – a proper gentleman this time, with a soft trace of Schwabing, without dialect. He, too, is very brief: one mustn't be used to "set an example," as that is always unjust. The tribunal withdraws and comes right back. The accused receives two days in prison, which have been served while awaiting trial. He also receives a reprimand. "Now get back to dealing in shoelaces and not ration stamps!" Though I am not a lawyer, I believe such a case would not previously have been handled very differently by juvenile, trade, or lay assessors' courts. But how much nicer it sounds to say "Revolutionary Tribunal"! . . . The second case is more serious. A soldier conducting "weapons checks" in bourgeois houses had taken a drink, gotten drunk, and, toward evening, aggressively threatened a bourgeois family with a revolver. The family phoned for help, terrified, and other soldiers arrived just as the accused was threatening to fire in the dark hallway. The chairman is gratifyingly gruff, and the sentence is six months in prison. Nothing can be said against the tribunal; it takes the sanctity of its affairs seriously. But the disastrous double-edged nature of the institution now becomes apparent. The audience mutters loudly. That was the kind of penalty you'd get under the old regime – there had been no need for a revolution, no need to overthrow the old judiciary, if a brave Red Guard was going to be so cruelly punished for intimidating the bourgeoisie a little bit! The tribunal has the unlimited power to impose sentences; there is no law to bind it, no professional training to give the judges a firm footing. And the omnipotence of this tribunal must turn into complete impotence at the given moment, in front of precisely this audience, the "sovereign" people . . .

Everywhere in Munich you find the same comedy, the same danger. I think people on the outside still imagine our situation to be more nightmarish than it is; this is still more of a game of revolution than a bloody revolution, there are still more Snug the Joiners walking around than actual lions – but at any hour it can change, and change dramatically. And the damage being done to Munich is already tremendous. I went to the train station to ask if mail could be sent to northern Germany. Where single guards once stood, there are now whole rows of armed men standing "cheek by jowl" in front of the porticos, most of them workers with a small tag on their lapel: "Maffei." Machine guns point menacingly from the windows above and from the roofs. I was told that one could drop letters in the box, and even registered letters were being accepted again, but no one could say whether or when they would be sent. And just as train and postal services have nearly stopped, so have all trade and industry in the city, for more than a week now. An outright general strike cannot take place; now and then posters appear explicitly excluding individual companies, individual lines of business, from striking. But everything stagnates more from day to day, and the vast majority of the population suffers more from day to day. As a special concession, the streetcars started up again over the holidays; they say the coffers of the ruling powers are completely empty and they had to get money from somewhere, because if the troops aren't paid, they will rally together – behind whom, I wonder? They always rally behind the person who pays them. The streetcar, they say, will bring in another few days of wages.

A soldier conducting drunken "weapons checks" in bourgeois houses – citizens had been ordered to hand in their weapons "under penalty of death" – had threatened a family with a revolver, the terrified family had phoned for help, and the soldiers who were sent in afterward had disarmed the dangerous ruffian. Sentence: six months in prison. It seemed almost too lenient to me, but during the break the audience muttered that they hadn't had a revolution and replaced educated civil servants with proletarian judges just so a hardworking soldier from the Red Army would have to sit in jail for half a year for such a triviality. This criticism made it clear to me that even the comedy of the gentle and staid tribunal with the bloodthirsty name was of a dangerous sort, just as dangerous as the Red Army's ludicrous lack of discipline. According to the new regulations, the punishments to be meted out were largely left to the discretion of the judges, who were expected to dispense popular justice. How long would it take before they yielded to the pressure of public sentiment and turned into a real revolutionary tribunal? No, I could not simply laugh at this toying with the Council Republic; it was abhorrent to me, and it was disquieting to me, even before it grew serious. But where could I place my sympathies? I had absolutely no time left for the Munich bourgeoisie. They seemed to be a totally apathetic mass. Day after day, whenever I passed by, I saw an old married couple leaning out of a window on Schellingstrasse. Each of the elderly couple had their own cushion, and they motionlessly observed what was happening below, even when nothing was happening. I am convinced that, with the exception of mealtimes, they reclined in their window from morning to evening, and that they had reclined with the same imperturbable, dull interest when it was not a revolution but still a war outside, and when, before the war, it was the peace of the white-and-blue kingdom. I viewed this married couple in the window as the very symbol of the Munich bourgeoisie. On that radiant Easter Sunday, Ludwigstrasse and Schellingstrasse were literally black with the thousands of people streaming out of Mass, and in the black throng were hundreds of luminous white dots: little girls dressed in white, holding their candles stiffly in front of them, coming from communion. Every few minutes you heard a shrill whistling. Then a military vehicle, red-pennanted and studded with machine guns, would race up recklessly fast. The crowd would push away from the middle road, the vehicle would shoot through, and the crowd would sluggishly flow together again. The Munich Council Republic and the Munich bourgeoisie seemed to have nothing to do with one another, and seemed to do each other no harm.

Easter Sunday, April 20, 1919

Communion and communism. Ludwigstrasse and Schellingstrasse are literally black with the thousands of people streaming out of Mass. And in the black throng, hundreds of little white dots (one could almost grow lyrical, if the times allowed, and speak of snowdrops in the black earth of spring): the little girls dressed in white, holding their candles stiffly in front of them, coming from communion. The crowd parts anxiously as a military vehicle, red-pennanted, studded with machine guns, races up with a whistle. Not a single day goes by that this reckless driving, which is just a lark, does not claim victims. This is how one dies for freedom! The driving is a lark, and the shooting, too. We now see lovely pheasant feathers stuck onto rifles like bayonets; the pheasants in the English Garden are very alluring prey. But whenever Franz Mair shoots pheasants in the English Garden, Xaver Huber on

Feilitzschplatz thinks the Whites are staging a coup, so he shoots, too, and then the guard at the nearby Church of the Redeemer rings the alarm bell, and soon there's the clatter of gunfire for a quarter of an hour all around. This is very amusing, especially for the youngsters; the children play "revolution" in the streets with red rags, and I know a very young boy who beams as he tries to speak his first words: "boom boom!" when the shotguns crack, and "ratatat!" when the machine guns rattle. But this lark, too, naturally claims victims every day, very often women and children.

The great pastime of shooting at planes, on the other hand – for which defensive artillery had even been stationed in the Hofgarten – has fallen out of fashion, at least for the time being. This has to do with an improvement in the situation of the local government. "The Schleissheim air detachment has rallied behind the Council Republic. They are doing their duty with red pennants. Shooting at aircraft is strictly forbidden." Immediately afterward, of course, a Bamberg flyer floated down, signed by Hoffmann–Schneppenhorst, entreating the people of Munich to persevere, as the government "knows of your suffering" and would bring help. But belief in this help has grown faint. One of Landauer's colleagues told me that this latest Council Republic was feeling more secure again. The 2nd and 3rd Army Corps had "rallied behind it" (this is the most popular expression after "anchoring"), the peasants in the region had been brought to heel by agitators and were supplying food once more; business could thus continue as usual. As it happens, comestibles are getting through again; the communists had threatened to let the bourgeoisie starve if the blockade continued. And now the intellect is to come into its own again as well: Levien will apparently tolerate Landauer at his side as Minister of Culture. I asked how the idealistic Landauer could hold office alongside the notoriously soft-headed and brutal "Minister of War." The response was that Gorky was working beneficially alongside Lenin in Russia, after all, and everyone was free in their own sphere in the Council Republic!

So we may yet have the pleasure of Landauer's grand reforms and debureaucratization. Incidentally, I heard of a nice prank played on him recently by the department heads on his first day in office, and this prank was personally confirmed by Landauer himself – though he had taken it seriously, as evidence of bureaucracy. Landauer had called for the department heads. He declared that from now on, as a true People's Deputy, he wanted to see everything for himself and sort it out simply and unbureaucratically. The next morning two laundry baskets stood on either side of his desk, full of incoming and outgoing mail with all of the corresponding bundles of files. A window sash had to be repaired in a convent school, the students at a secondary school wanted to establish a soccer club – all of this, with all of its documentary material, was presented to the People's Deputy. In despair, he called for the department heads again. Had all of this landed on the desk of the minister under the old regime too? No, it had been handled by the different departments, but Herr Landauer – he had done away with the title, of

course – had expressly ordered . . . Well, now he was ordering everything to be done as it was before! So, ultimately, this reform could take on characteristics similar to that of the court system. But here, too, the threat of chaos looms, and the child's play can descend into total destruction.

And if flyers are the only help that Herr Hoffmann sends, then destruction is bound to come.

The people of Munich will not help themselves. One of the new second-ranking leaders, a keen agitator[189] and staunch friend of the people, recently revealed to me – half-unwittingly – his real opinion, real estimation of the Bavarians. "We Badeners and northern Germans have to lead. The people are undiscriminating and lazy in and of themselves. But now we preach to them every day: you were the first to throw out the king, to have your Eisner, and now you must continue to be the first revolutionaries, to have the first council republic! And by appealing to your ambition like this, we can achieve anything!"

Hopes are sinking, and one already hears people saying that Hoffmann's government, that

Bavaria, will not be able to provide any help at all of its own accord. Now a rumor has been circulating since yesterday in this utterly newspaperless city that troops from Württemberg are on the march and will bring help. On the street, on the joyously welcomed streetcar, in the salons, the bourgeoisie and ordinary people are saying it, whispering anxiously, half believing, half unbelieving. And all of them add: "As long as they ain't Prussians!"

Easter Monday, April 21, 1919

Tranquil comings and goings in the English Garden: parents and children and countless "doggies" and couples upon couples on every avenue and every bench. Where else can they go? No one dares venture into the surrounding countryside; they keep saying the Whites are about to attack. And the train can only be used by those who have proof of three months' membership in the U.S.P. or the Spartacus League! Bikes, too, are very often "confiscated" by the guards. Suddenly a machine gun crackles close by. No one jumps. "Shootin' pheasants again!" All pleasures are for the "working people." The latest poster even reserves the National Theater for them: "Tickets will only be issued upon presentation of work passes." And sedately, delighted with this renewed world, already entirely accustomed to its strange novelty, the bourgeoisie goes for a stroll.

April 22, 1919

Thou shalt remember the third Sabbath day, to keep it holy! After a two-day break, the bakeries were allowed to sell again until 10 o'clock. Then it was: "Close everything. Last day of the general strike. The city is being decked with red flags; the workers' battalions will parade past the Ministry of War at 11, a general demonstration will be held at 5." I witnessed both. The march of the battalions was good, insofar as it was not soldiers who were marching. The troops are young lads who look bold but unmartial, none of whom have ever smelled gunpowder. But the civilians! They are the actual soldiers; they present themselves and hold their weapons no differently than they did when they took up position outside. Firmness of stance, determined faces. A few stand out on account of their age or deformities, others on account of a particular bitterness in their expression. But they all have composure. If it does come to combat, the workers will fight and the soldiers will run. As strong as the morning parade appeared – in its civilian parts, anyway, which were the actual military parts – with its few thousand people (of the purported 45,000 workers, perhaps a tenth marched past Minister of War Levien), the larger afternoon demonstration descended into the typical revelry. Once again it filed down Ludwigstrasse, this time with masses of people, armed and unarmed, men, women, half-grown boys, with the loveliest red flags, fabulously jolly, especially the girls. Every few minutes a marshal shouted an "up" or a "down" and then they all roared merrily, jubilantly, with all their might, and they threw their arms in the air, and the boldest even brandished their weapons over their heads. The drawn-out "downs" sounded especially nice. "Down with the Hohenzollern socialists, dowwwn, dowwwn, dowwwn!" – Tomorrow everyone is supposed to work again, and the Württembergers are supposed to actually be advancing, and some people hope that the local ruling powers will give in and capitulate. Perhaps today was their farewell performance?

A.B.

But then the situation did grow more serious – for both sides. That Tuesday was probably the last day of untarnished fun. The period before had been full of strikes, though never a complete general strike, even though the government had proclaimed one. The discontinued streetcar operations had been especially bothersome. They had been allowed to run over Easter; the city-state's money was depleted and this was a good source of revenue. Now they said: "Last day of the general strike; the city is being decked with red flags; the workers' battalions will parade past the Ministry of War at 11, a general demonstration will be held at 5." I witnessed both of them. The march of the battalions was good, insofar as it was not soldiers who were marching. The workers in civilian garb, older people with serious, often embittered faces, carried rifles and deported themselves no differently than they had when they took up position outside. The soldiers, on the other hand, were young boys who clearly took the whole thing to be a bit of cheeky fun. "If it actually turns serious," I wrote, "the workers will fight and the soldiers will run." But during the large afternoon demonstration, I was more convinced than ever that it would not turn serious! What a carnival. In the morning a few thousand had marched past, but now a huge mass filed down Ludwigstrasse with countless fluttering red flags, armed and unarmed, men and women and girls and boys, all of them chatting blithely and shouting with all their might when the marshals called for a cheer for the Council Republic, and roaring even more merrily when it was a "down!" – "Down with the Hohenzollern socialists!" They threw their arms in the air, and the boldest waved their rifles above their heads. And then they sang and then they chatted some more – no, it wouldn't turn serious, it was just a game. And perhaps this was the farewell performance of the fanciful government, because a rumor was now circulating that Reich troops were advancing in large numbers. Surely the government would give in and capitulate in good time. – And then it turned serious indeed. The situation deteriorated in the following days. Food grew scarce, looting increased, more shots were fired, alarm bells rang more often. Only the widespread shooting at planes from Bamberg was strictly forbidden, and this had to do with a military advantage on the part of the Council Republic. It now had planes itself, which were not to be confused with enemy planes; the Schleissheim air detachment had "rallied behind it." How often did I hear this fashionable expression that year: troops, communities, clubs rallied behind a government, a party, a resolution, behind the most important things and the most trivial, rallied behind Red one day and behind White the next. Only one other expression was encountered as often at the time: the Bavarian safeguards would, as they say now, be "anchored in the constitution," as was declared by the Democratic delegate Quidde, whom I heard speak before his fellow Munich party members about the work of the National Assembly just prior to proclamation of the Council Republic. Rallying behind something and anchoring something – the full yearning of divided and uprooted millions is expressed in these two catchwords, which very soon not only grew trite, but actually took on ominously contradictory meanings: those who rallied behind something were definitely unreliable, and whatever had been "anchored" would definitely not remain in place. Incidentally, the Bavarian safeguards, whose anchoring Quidde had promised to Munich's Liberals, were a substitute for the old reserved rights[190] that were officially frowned upon in both wording and substance. "You need not insist on a Bavarian Ministry of War – you must not, in fact, because otherwise the Prussians will then demand a special Prussian Ministry of War, and that would result in the old Prussian domination," the man had to say to pacify his people. This was the strength of the narrow-minded particularism even among the small, progressive part of the Bavarian bourgeoisie. No, I could not warm to this bourgeoisie, at least, any more than I could to the Spartacists. And once the bourgeoisie began to realize that the council republican game they had watched half-apathetically, half-sullenly to that point could actually mean something worse for them than just a wild, carnivalistic performance, how did they demonstrate their awakening to resistance? Through spontaneous anti-Semitism. "Jewish pigs!" ranted individuals in front of the posters on the walls, "Jewish pigs!" roared the occasional small chorus, and flyers appeared blaming the Jews entirely for the Council Republic, for the revolution itself, for inciting the war, for its disastrous outcome. The only difference between the flyers and the speeches in the streets was that the flyers held the Jews alone responsible for everything, while in common bourgeois parlance Jews were mentioned alongside Prussians – and in such close alliance that Jew and Prussian often sounded like synonyms for the same principle of evil.

Where could I place my sympathies? They most naturally belonged to my circle of university colleagues, who stood up for the cohesion of the Fatherland, for internal peace and order, if only because then Germany would not be all too helpless in its peace negotiations with the Entente. But even on the academic side, there was no shortage of attachments that appealed very little to me. How odd it was to witness the boundless jubilation of a student assembly in the main auditorium when the first consolatory flyer from the Bamberg government was announced. With the exception of a very tiny group, the students were neither socialist nor liberal – if it had been up to them, Germany would probably have regained a monarchy and a very conservative constitution. And how they roared with delight because the Majority Socialist government of the Free State of Bavaria had shown signs of life. Still, the humor of this outburst had something touching about it. For them, the weak Socialist prime minister Hoffmann embodied the order of the Reich as compared to the devilment of the Council Republic. How excruciating it was to sit through the long, dithering back-and-forth of the professors before they finally agreed (after a good deal of speechifying, I must say) to resign jointly if the Council Republic should prevent any one of them from lecturing, and how lukewarm they were as a whole toward Weimar. Nonetheless, through Easter and beyond I felt very connected to the academics. And then anti-Semitism began to run rampant here, too, and for the mass of students the Jew became a convenient, all-purpose enemy, and it never occurred to the majority of professors to counter the rising anti-Semitism. I do not want to exaggerate: there were a good many lecturers and students in Munich at the time who very much condemned this eruption of hostility toward Jews, and during my entire time in Munich I was never personally subjected to anti-Semitism, but I did feel depressed and isolated by it. And it was right at this time that the feeling of isolation I so dearly wanted to escape was intensified most painfully from another side. In March, the poor Sonja Lerch had been resurrected – barely changed on the outside, very much changed on the inside – in the form of her older sister. The first time Lydia Rabinowitz[191] visited us in the company of Lerch, we nearly got a fright to see how much she resembled the deceased. We also both immediately had the impression that Lerch had sought and found comfort in her. With her hard eyes and her all-too-confident manner, I found Lydia Rabinowitz rather unlikeable from the outset, but she behaved impeccably toward us, and she was not uninteresting. She boasted of having tried a dozen professions and pursued various studies, particularly art history and medicine; she was a divorcée and had a ten-year-old son somewhere in Switzerland, and she now wanted to train as a rhythmic gymnastics teacher. After getting along passably well for several weeks, the four of us even meeting once at Vossler's, I ran into her in the busy hall of the university shortly after Easter. I approached her with an outstretched hand and said, "We haven't seen each other for a week, why don't you and Lerch come by our boarding house?" She refused my hand, stared at me stonily and said loudly enough for everyone around us to hear: "I've heard you're playing the Protestant. I don't associate with converted Jews." And then she turned her back on me. That evening we were supposed to visit Vossler, where we found "Lerchs," as we called the two of them. My wife and I chatted with Vossler and Lerch over the head of Rabinowitz, who was sitting in between, as if her chair were empty; it must have been very obvious. We soon left, and downstairs I said, "Now they'll have at me." The next day, outside the work room, there were embarrassing confrontations first with Vossler, then with Lerch. Vossler said Rabinowitz was a fanatical Zionist and all fanatics rubbed him the wrong way, but Rabinowitz was very much in favor with Lerch, and he needed Lerch (a need that I will come back to). Rabinowitz had apparently published an article in the *Bayrischer Kurier*, according to which the Germans were lacking in anti-Semitism, and she viewed all Jews who professed their Germanness to be traitors. Lerch came afterward, half wanting to intercede, half wanting to intimidate me, and both things upset me equally. He said "converted Jew" wasn't an insult that warranted such harsh retaliation on my part; his sister-in-law was now proposing a kind of religious discussion, and if I refused, she would publicly call me to account. I refused any debate with her and warned Lerch of the consequences of any further attack by his sister-in-law, both for her and for him. In fact, I had no idea what those consequences might be, or what

I should do if the rabid Rabinowitz were to abuse me during a lecture in front of the students. But Lerch must have gotten worried and had enough of the sensation caused by his first wife, so it seems he kept her sister in check – nothing more happened, in any case. We carefully avoided one another, and Vossler's subsequent invitations tended to be along the lines of: "Lerch was here yesterday – the coast will be clear."

In the meantime, the Council Republic was rapidly coming to an end. For a moment it once again looked as though the conclusion would be a bloodlessly absurd one. After the end of the general strike, newspapers could be published again – with prior censorship, of course. The *Post* reported on a meeting in which the People's Deputies had given an account of the status of their departments. The food minister had declared that his supplies could last another fourteen days if he didn't have to give anything to the bourgeoisie. The finance minister[192] had declared that he could last just about as long if the paper factory in Dachau wasn't lost to the enemy. Nothing more could be gotten out of the paper factory because Hoffmann's government had taken all of the embossing stamps, with the exception of those for one-mark and fifty-pfennig bills. Levien had consequently resigned as chairman, and now negotiations with Bamberg could begin. And while not everything aspired to by the Council Republic had been achieved, they thought they had at least done the preparatory, educational, and beneficial work that was in keeping with its goals.

April 30, 1919

Today it finally looks as though we will be liberated at last from this ludicrous and senseless Hell we have inhabited since April 7th, and its lower circles since the 13th. Yesterday evening there was an especially urgent alarm, with the usual bells and gunshots accompanied by steam sirens in the factories, the prominent rumble of trains, which were apparently moving out reinforcements (because no trains are running otherwise, and the postal service stopped carrying anything beyond Dachau long ago), and distant cannon blasts which lasted through the night and remained audible even during the day. And then came two ominous posters, one listing a number of casualty stations set up in Munich, the other bearing the headline: "Guards Cavalry Rifle Division from Berlin outside Munich." It reported that the "murderers of Luxemburg and Liebknecht" had been unleashed on Munich and were shooting prisoners in heaps, even medics, even defenseless old people, and their identity papers were "signed by Noske." "Noske now plans to perpetrate a bloodbath among the unified Munich proletariat. Workers! Soldiers! Shake off Prussian domination!" The most interesting thing about this poster, which once again agitated for the Red Army, was the reaction of the public. Some laughed, some ranted – but not at the Prussians. "If only they would come and finally liberate us from this rabble!" But it was also impossible not to notice that a half-dull, half-melancholy sense of disbelief was mixed with these feelings of rage and hope. After much observation, I am sure I am right in saying that the emotional state of the Munich majority is currently one of weary resignation. They tell themselves there is no hope of real relief; one way or another, everything will continue to muddle along. This outlook very clearly has two roots. First, there is no longer any faith in the strength, and now only very little faith in the goodwill, of Hoffmann's government "outside." All too often its planes told us that help was on the way, and nothing happened. Now people are saying the government won't manage on its own, with insecure Bavarian troops, and it won't risk bringing in foreign troops, much less Prussian ones. (And yet that would no longer be a risk, they would be received like saviors here by the bourgeoisie and petite bourgeoisie and even most of the workers, who are now just unwilling pawns in this lunatic game!) But our resignation is also rooted in the weakness of our local "government," which has long ceased to be one. Everyone knows it can no longer survive, and they fear negotiations. Negotiations between two weak parties lead to lazy compromises which, after a brief peace, are followed by new acts of violence

1. Klemperer's career as the "A.B. correspondent" for the *Leipziger Neueste Nachrichten* began in Café Merkur in Leipzig. When all of the lights went out at home due to strikes, the Merkur went "from a café to a refuge."

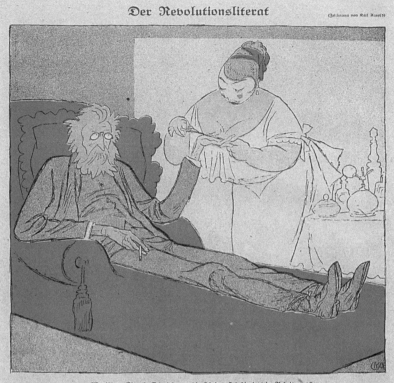

Der Revolutionsliterat

„Maniküren Sie mir Schwielen an die Hände. Ich bin jetzt im Arbeiterrat."

2. The caricature that Klemperer discussed with the journalist Paul Harms: "'That fits perfectly with your account of Eisner and the "Council of Intellectual Workers,"' Harms said after we had laughed long enough over the picture. 'You really should write reports for us from Munich.'"

3. Erich Mühsam, 1918.

4. Kurt Eisner, first prime minister of the Bavarian revolutionary government formed on November 8, 1918, "and his rapt audience – I had to keep reminding myself of this – was not a heap of literary 'intellectual workers,' but literally the people of Munich," Klemperer noted in 1942.

5. Eisner and his wife, Else, at a demonstration for the Munich councils system on
February 16, 1919.

6. From February 7, 1919, Victor Klemperer worked as a university lecturer at Ludwig-Maximilian University in Munich, teaching students returning home from the war.

7. The Council of People's Deputies, December 1918, considered by the revolutionaries to be "the bloodhounds in Berlin": Philipp Scheidemann, Chancellor (2nd from left); Gustav Noske, Reich Minister of Defense (center); Friedrich Ebert, President of the Reich government formed on February 13, 1919 (2nd from right).

München nach Eisners Ermordung.

(Von unserem A.B.-Mitarbeiter)

München, 22. Febr.

Der lebendige und der tote Eisner. — Die "zweite Revolution" — Graf, Korpsstudent und Offizier. — Peinliche Ungemütlichkeit. — Das Stadtbild. — Die "Leiber". — Auf der Theresienwiese. — Die beunruhigenden Krieger. — Die vergewaltigte Preßfreiheit. — Der verschwundene Landtag. — Auer.

8. "The mood is Descartes-esque. The only certainty is that everything is in doubt," Klemperer wrote in his report "Munich After Eisner's Assassination," which was published on February 24, 1919.

9. Kurt Eisner's funeral on February 26, 1919, at the Ostfriedhof in Munich, turned into one of the largest revolutionary protest rallies. In the middle of the crowd is the coach carrying Else Eisner.

10. Gustav Noske, who used extreme brutality to crush the councils experiment, in his office, 1919.

11. On April 30, 1919, Klemperer noted: "Some time ago *Simplicissimus* published a picture of a Berlin family reciting its 'Pater Noske'; how many, many thousands of people here long for such a Pater Noske."

12. In Munich, left-wing radicals proclaimed the Council Republic on April 7, 1919. Two days later, Klemperer wrote: "Landauer [...] appears to me to be Eisner reincarnate, not one bit smarter, but a good bit more radical."

13. After just one week, the pacifist intellectuals were booted out and a Second Council Republic was proclaimed. Klemperer viewed Max Levien, the man of the hour, as a "brutal 'minister of war.'"

14. Red Army soldiers near the Stachus square with mortars, hand grenades and ammunition boxes, 1919.

15. "The Stachus had a wildly romantic look about it. In the middle of the square a little shop had been gutted by fire and the advertising pillars next to it shattered by a grenade."

16. Government soldiers on Marienplatz. After the fighting, Victor Klemperer noted on May 10, 1919: "Munich is not in a festive mood, there is only concern and depression on the one side, terrible acrimony on the other. The fight was all too furious, and the desperate resistance of the communists surpassed all expectations."
'DE-1992-FS-REV-170 – Stadtarchiv München'

by the more unscrupulous party. Some time ago *Simplicissimus* published a picture of a Berlin family reciting its "Pater Noske"; how many, many thousands of people here long for such a Pater Noske, whether his name is Epp or something else. Only a stricter reckoning could help us, and no one really dares hope for it any more, despite the Berlin Guards Riflemen, whose actual presence at the gates is impossible for us to confirm, after all. – –

The weakness of the local rulers – whom no one really knows any more because they switch positions every six to twelve hours – has become ever more comically apparent since the big demonstration marking the end of the general strike. On the 27th the *Post*, which could now be published again, reported on a meeting of the workers' councilors, during which the individual "People's Deputies" gave an account of the situation. The representative of the Provisions Office said they could last another fourteen days as long as they didn't have to give anything to the civilian population. But they knew the civilian population is entirely out of milk and fat, and has almost no more meat. Finance Minister Maenner, on the other hand, made the happy announcement that they could last another four weeks financially "if the White Guards don't capture the paper factory in Dachau." And even the paper factory in Dachau can only provide meager resources because it only has printing plates for two-, one- and half-mark bills; the other printing materials were taken away by Hoffmann's government!

The outcome of this meeting on the 27th was that Comrade Levien resigned, a more moderate line gained the upper hand (though no one knew to what extent or for how long), bourgeois newspapers were released with prior censorship, and the ruling powers wearily declared that they would negotiate, and that even if they had not yet managed to fully implement the council idea, they had at least done a few weeks of "educational" work. But immediately afterward, the *Rote Fahne* called for all-out resistance and cursed all traitors, and we heard of new hostages being taken, and severe punishments were threatened for anyone who spoke ill of

Comrade Levien in particular or the Council Republic in general. The ease with which one can find oneself facing such punishment was demonstrated to me by a close and somewhat adventurous acquaintance who has a few Schwabing friends. He passes by the Wittelsbach Palace, the seat of the government. Someone shouts at him: "Hey, friend – why aren't you serving our cause?!" The counterquestion: Since when do people address each other so informally, and how could one be of use? The answer: We communists all address each other informally here, and you can certainly be of use to us. Friend H.[193] is taken to a room where, without further ado, he is given a nicely stamped identity card, which he happily showed to me. "Committee for Combating the Counter-revolution. Comrade H. has the right to bear arms and make arrests that he believes are necessary in the interest of the revolution." In the course of the conversation, he first said he could easily get the same certificate for me, then later threatened to arrest me if I didn't give him a cigarette. What was just a joke between us

could be serious in many other cases, and is often enough deadly serious.

The *Staatszeitung*, the only bourgeois newspaper to take advantage of the kind permission granted to it, appeared on the 28th. Its supplement contained a very characteristic joke. In its official section it published the notices of the various State Ministries (of the Interior, of Culture, of Agriculture, and Forestry) from the start to the end of April, each of the orders having been duly signed by the department heads working in Munich. The fact that the ministries had been abolished, the department heads dismissed, and the institutions affected by these orders entirely turned around through the many decrees issued by a constant stream of new people's deputies and workers' councils and revolutionary committees – the good department heads had paid this no mind and had instead stayed where they were, and kept working, and kept waiting.

It was less amusing to read external newspapers, a few of which have been arriving irregularly after long delays since the end of the general strike (while letter mail has stopped altogether). We have caught sight of copies of the *Reichszeitung* that were seven to eight days old, and somewhat more freshly baked copies of the *Wiener Zeitung*. They said that Lettow-Vorbeck[194] was on the march and "Munich was set to fall," which we believed all the less given that flyers dropped from a plane on the 25th had ordered us to be home by six in the evening because the battle was starting – and then, once again, everything had remained calm. –

It was not these unfulfilled prophecies that we found most disagreeable, however, but the horror stories that had been spread about Munich. An appalling amount of blood is supposed to have been spilled already, houses are supposed to have gone up in flames, and the communists are supposed to have begun communizing the women and girls of the bourgeoisie. Not a word of this is true (to date, anyway); to date, the communists have refrained from pointless bestiality. Now they boast, of course, saying that the bourgeois press lies, and they'll show the misguided troops what

fine people the communists are; this way they'll get the troops to desert, as they recently managed to do during their great victory in Dachau. And I honestly fear that the communists could whitewash themselves this way and thus conceal the accumulated injustices they have on their conscience. Because while they may not yet have committed murder and not yet burned Munich to ashes, they have certainly not refrained from doing everything else that must inevitably wean the unrestrained mass from a sense of justice and gradually, ultimately, lead to the worst crimes. Arbitrary arrests, hostage-taking, house searches that degenerate into the basest looting, and always, always, incitement of the worst, bloodiest, most heinous kind against the now defenseless, completely disenfranchised, completely browbeaten populace. If the "Prussians" really do attack tomorrow – who will vouch for the safety of the hostages, for the long-gone inviolability of private property? But the "Prussians" will not come, and we will negotiate with Herr Hoffmann, and the Augean stable, which the Munich native refers to frankly as a "pigsty," will perhaps get some fresh air and a connection with the outside world through the crack in the door, but it is unlikely to be cleaned out.

[. . .] I walked along Ludwigstrasse for quite a while.[195] It was the same all over: people spoke with revulsion about the murder of the hostages and with satisfaction about the liberators, and they took not the slightest exception to the fact that the liberators were said to be Prussians. No sooner had I gotten home, at about eleven, than a few shots were fired nearby, followed immediately by the clatter of a toppling bicycle. I ran to the window and saw a Red Guard standing next to the bike, and an elderly gentleman gripping him by the arm, and a young man who tore the cartridge-studded scarf from his neck; the gun lay next to the bike at the edge of the sidewalk. The Guard broke free and ran away, stripping off his red armband as he ran. That was the start of the bourgeois counter-revolution.

I went out again, since now I was on duty as A.B. On April 8th Harms had asked me for news by telegraph, and since then I had been keeping a revolutionary diary. I had only been able to send off the start of it, of course; all the rest had been saved up, but now the path would be clear again. When I reached Ludwigstrasse, everything was calm. The blue-and-white flag fluttered over the Ministry of War, blue-and-white fluttered next to red over the Residence, and over the Wittelsbach Palace (a central point for the Council Republic) there was a white cloth. Civilians, most likely students and former officers judging from their look, a rifle or revolver in hand, a white band, handkerchief, or piece of bandage around the arm, hurried along singly or in small groups, I don't know where to. Even soldiers from the garrison wore white armbands, though yesterday they had still "rallied" behind the Council Republic and worn red ones. This reversal had come quick as a flash, although there was not yet any sign of an invasion by Reich troops. The Spartacists must have been completely destroyed. It was early afternoon when the victors finally moved in. Today it is a commonplace and utterly untruthful newspaper cliché to say that incoming conquerors are "cheered as liberators by the rescued population." But regarding the arrival of these troops in Munich on May 1, 1919, there is really no other way I can put it. Bavarian heavy cavalry rode in, and Württemberg dragoons with black-and-red pennants, and Epp's Freikorps men with the golden lion's head in a black diamond on their upper arms, and Prussians with the white death's head of the Potsdam hussars on their caps. And all of them were greeted with cheers and waving handkerchiefs, and they were given cigarettes and cigars. It turned into a proper festival in front of the university, where Prussian troops had been billeted for the moment. For the first and only time in my life – the glory lasted all of two days – I witnessed a joyous Bavarian-Prussian brotherhood. Men, women, and children had climbed on top of the Siegestor, where they crouched picturesquely on the team of lions and waved flags, waved their hands and shouted. Around the semicircle in front of the university, into which vehicles and a captured cannon had been driven, the people of Munich jostled and chatted with the guards and the soldiers standing around doing nothing – it was the most droll collision of Berlinese and Munichese.[196] [. . .]

May 2, 1919

So steps have actually been taken to clean things out after all. But sadly, the tremendous jubilation that created a real May Day holiday here yesterday, especially in the afternoon – though a very different holiday from the one dreamed of by the "socialist youth," the "fourteen- to eighteen-year-olds" who wanted to protest en masse against all backward governments, among whom they counted the local councils, a holiday where Bavarians cheered on Prussians and hard-bitten anti-militarists cheered on stern soldiers and even (*horribile dictu!*)[197] officers with proper epaulets, with steel helmets and squad rifles too, of course – this delighted jubilation died down in the evening and has not really managed to build up again today, even though thousands of handkerchiefs are still wafted at the steady stream of incoming troops. This is because since the afternoon, and all through the night, and now for all of Friday, the most bitter fighting has raged continuously, growing from a skirmish to a slaughter, and the blast of mines and grenades shudders the earth almost non-stop and drowns out the wild rattle of machine-gun fire and the crack of gunshots. A great deal of blood is flowing in the inner city, where the Spartacists are desperately holding their ground, as they likely have nothing to gain from surrender anymore.

The morning of May 1st was the last time it looked as though the city of Munich itself would be spared any street fighting. Two posters have taken the place of newspapers for us again. A general strike had been declared once more the previous day, but without being altogether heeded by the despairing owners of small shops. One poster expressed the government's outrage at the murder of the hostages that was committed overnight. It said the government was blameless. Blameless, after agitating for so long, blameless, after delivering the defenseless people to the systematically brutalized mob! At the moment we still do not even know the names of all those killed, as their bodies are hideously mutilated. But that a railroad secretary and a secondary-school teacher were among these "capitalists" and "aristocrats," and a woman as well – that much we do know. There is also talk of Döderlein,[198] the brilliant gynecologist who helped so many people. . . On the second poster, the blameless government explained that it looked as though the council's idea would be trampled by raw military might. But it said that an idea cannot die (it can only murder!), and as a sign of this, the workers and soldiers were asked to demonstrate unarmed on the Theresienwiese. The "unarmed" was heavily emphasized, making the entire thing looked like frightened capitulation, and the rage expressed everywhere at the shameful murder[199] was clearly mixed with a feeling of relief and gratification: everyone said the Ostbahnhof had been taken by Prussians in the night, and the liberating troops would move in without a fight in a few hours. Then, at about 11 p.m., a clatter rises up from Ludwigstrasse, and frightened people run past under my window on the neighboring Schellingstrasse. Immediately after, an unsuspecting Red Guard cycles up and is pulled from his bike, an elderly gentleman tears off his ammunition pouch in a single move, a young man pulls his rifle over his head, takes his cartridge-studded scarf as well, knocks off his cap and leaves the dumbfounded guard standing there. That was the start of the "counter-revolution" here. When I reached the street, this first flurry of activity was already over. In its speed, it had had a tremendous effect. A white-and-blue flag was already waving above the Ministry of War, the white-and-blue waved over the red on the Residence, and above the Wittelsbach Palace there was a white cloth. All of this was in the hands of the Whites? Where had they come from so mysteriously quickly? Because there were not yet any external troops in Munich, and the bourgeoisie had been completely disarmed. But apparently not so completely. Some had been able to hide their guns and were now hauling them out again. And then the troops. The pioneers here had always been the problem children of the soviet people: students, merchants,

bourgeoisie – they conspire, they wait for their moment. And the Lifeguards – well, the Lifeguards had once again declared themselves to be "neutral," so neutral that one could fetch weapons from their barracks. It was very, very strange. The Red Guard who was disarmed outside my window was the last man I saw with a red armband; from then on I only encountered soldiers with white bands, often hastily cobbled together from bandage material. But more often than soldiers, one encountered civilians with the look of students and even former officers, judging partially from their faces, partially from their pristine, high leather gaiters. They had simply wrapped a handkerchief around their arm, slung a rifle over their shoulder. Occasionally a revolver peeked out of a coat pocket or was held in the hand, ready to fire. The few armed people were usually accompanied by a train of unarmed people, young and old, sometimes with workers among the bourgeoisie. And each of these trains brandished a white-and-blue pennant, and wherever they passed by, exultant faces appeared in the windows, handkerchiefs waved, flags – white-and-blue, not red! – were thrust out, it was like the wake of a great victory, like a peaceable public festival. And the festivities escalated even more. In the early afternoon the first troops rode in: Bavarian heavy cavalry moving down Barer Strasse. They hadn't received such a greeting when they returned home from the campaigns. But the festival reached its peak at the Siegestor and in front of the neighboring university, which is separated from the street by a wide semi-circle. Prussian troops marched in here and took temporary quarter in the university itself. Men, women, and children had climbed on top of the Siegestor, where they waved their hands, waved a flag, crouched picturesquely on the team of lions. Underneath the archway and around the guards in front of the semicircle, into which vehicles and a captured cannon had been driven, the people jostled and chatted with the soldiers and gave them cigarettes and never tired of the questions and the tales. And in the crowd, you heard over and over again: "Sure they're Prussians, but they're our libera-tors, too." One of the guards, a Potsdam death's-head hussar with many medals, a steel helmet on his head, and free cigarette behind his ear, explained in pure Berlin dialect that they were all volunteers and they knew of the hullabaloo from Berlin and elsewhere, and that some of them were old men, foresters with gray beards down to their bellies, but man, do they put a jerk in it! (What'd he say?), and that they'd come from Berlin two days ago, and they'd given the Spartacists a thrashing near Schleissheim, and that's where the howitzer was from, and it was a lot nicer here in Munich than they'd've thought, folks weren't the least bit hostile – just the opposite! Quite the opposite. You could imagine you had gone back to better times; indeed, you could almost hold out hope for better future times; so cordial was the interaction between civilians and the military here, and – it bears constant repeating – between burghers and Prussian officers. Every single person was greeted with waves and looks and shouts, and with cigarettes, and there was no end to the thanks and jubila-tion. But then you remembered the reason for this patriotic excitement – the communist rule here, the wretched role of the bourgeoisie, the weakness of the old government, which had truly not triumphed under its own power after all – and all sorts of acrimony tempered the joyful atmosphere.

From four o'clock onward we were reminded more and more of the seriousness of the situation. Munich was still far from being conquered; the communists held the inner city. While a jolly stream of people flooded Ludwigstrasse and, with great satisfaction, read the poster from Hoffmann's government – according to which Bavarian troops under General von Möhl[200] and Prussians under Lieutenant Colonel Oven[201] had marched in solely to restore order, and which simultaneously announced martial law and the provision of trains with food and coal – increasingly powerful detonations sounded in increasingly rapid succession. I later took a walk in the direction of the Stachus square to get my bearings. Huddles of people everywhere who recoiled when the wailing and crashing came all too close, only to poke their noses out again afterward; a few who were undaunted or for some reason compelled to advance further; black smoke in the vicinity of the train station. And more and more troops with colored steel helmets, establishing cordons, making for the battleground. In the evening we heard troops singing as they marched, like in 1914. The blasts had still not stopped, but everyone was hoping for calm the following day. Another 35,000 men were expected to arrive, and resistance – with an entire army sitting in Munich and nine-tenths of Munich cheering the liberators (and this cheering is not a newspaper cliché nor the lie of a bourgeois rag, after having seen it hundreds of times and comparing it with the reception given to the Council Republic and its demonstrations, I can swear to it!) – resistance was now pointless. Nonetheless: all through the day and late into the afternoon, as I write these lines, a thunderous battle has raged. An entire squadron of planes is crisscrossing Munich, directing fire, drawing fire itself, dropping flares; bombs and grenades blast constantly, sometimes farther away, sometimes nearer, shaking the houses, and a torrent of machine-gun fire follows the explosions, with infantry fire rattling in between. And all the while new troops march, drive, ride down Ludwigstrasse with mortars, artillery, forage wagons, and field kitchens, sometimes accompanied by music, and a medical train has stopped at the Siegestor, and heavy patrols and various weapons divisions are scattering through the streets, and crowds of people form on every corner that provides cover but also a view, often with opera glasses in their hands. Whenever a man appears with the *Post*, shoves turn to blows as people fight for the scarce copies. I still haven't been able to get one. And if anyone arouses suspicion (he has a Spartacus card! or he still sympathizes with the Reds – well, my friend, we'll have no more of that), someone immediately runs to the nearest patrol with tales of assault or denunciations, and in the case of the most aggressive patriots, one could almost swear that just yesterday they were wearing the red armband instead of the white or white-and-blue. And then someone is arrested, and everyone's attention is drawn

to this intermezzo – until the next resounding blast, which reminds them all of the battle again.

Well, it cannot rage much longer; the resistance must be literally crushed, and tomorrow will likely involve mopping-up operations at most. But this is also what everything will come down to, because I would not advise Hoffmann's ministry to trust in a changed armband on the part of either the garrison or the "class-conscious" Independents and Spartacists. Already today I have heard people from the soviet idealists' camp, those supporting Landauer – who had nothing good to expect from either Hoffmann or Levien, and who has already been arrested – I have already heard these incorrigible ideologues saying that the maladministration that has just collapsed meant nothing, that the true Council Republic (which let us slip so effortlessly, so blamelessly effortlessly, into this very mishmash of ludicrousness and criminality!) will celebrate its resurrection three days after Noske's guards march off. I believe three measures are necessary to prevent this. The first is self-evident, the second is at least as necessary, and the third is the most important. The first is disarmament, the total disarmament of the communists and Independents; the second, a civil militia; and the third, the resignation of Hoffmann, who owes greater apologies to every party, and I mean every single party, than it is possible to offer *in politicis*. They say Auer is doing fairly well again.[202] And might it not be possible to find another fellow among the Bavarian bourgeoisie, at least one? Then the third man could come from the peasantry.

But we do need three men: a solid Majority Socialist, a Democrat who will remain at his post even when there's trouble, and a "Black" who knows exactly what the peasants and Catholic citizens of Bavaria want. And if we don't get this kind of coalition, then no military support from the Reich and no military dictatorship will help us, whether it lasts for eight days or eight weeks and is led by a Bavarian or a non-Bavarian general.

A.B.

May 4, 1919

Gunfire still crackles somewhere, from a side street one moment, from nearby roofs the next; you still hear a "clear the street!" and then people run, though certainly not nearly as fearfully quickly as in the first two days of fighting. Everyone has simply gotten used to the state of things, the street fights flaring up here and there, the moving barricades, the martial grotesquerie of life. What previously would have been an experience worthy of countless retellings is now casually taken

for granted. The peculiar arrival of more and more new troops: first, steel-helmeted infantrymen march in two long lines up against the rows of houses, covering each other, ready to fire, ordering windows to be shut whenever something strikes them as suspicious; then, following at a good distance, the artillery, train, medics, all the ordnance and equipment, even the helmets painted with dull patches of color. The jumble of tribes: along with Prussians and Bavarians – Epp's corps has moved in as well – there are now many Württembergers here, and the black-and-red pennants of their lancers flutter decoratively. The friendly but insistent demand for identification in manifold dialects on various street corners. . . All of this is now a matter of course. And only the center of the actual combat activity, the Stachus square and the area around the train station, is visited and discussed in detail by many thousands. And what if that were no longer an attraction either! The burned-out little shop in the middle of the square, the advertising pillars next to it, in the midst of which a grenade landed, the demolished roof beams of the big Mathäser building, the countless white bullet marks on the gray houses, especially on the Palace of Justice, which had a hole shot in its cupola, the bullet-riddled window panes, the grenade scars on the square tower of the Protestant church and the rubble in the plaza behind it, a pierced rain gutter, a shattered lamp post, and everywhere the ragged snarl of dangling wires. And among all of this, soldiers in combat gear everywhere, and machine guns

everywhere, the long bullet belt inserted and ready for use, and if you approach a harmless truck advertising itself as belonging to a cheese or butter wholesaler, you'll find it also carries a combat-ready machine gun. No cinema could offer more of a sensation. And always, always, the flaring crackle of gunfire. And the excited public itself stokes the marvelous sensation to superlative levels. Discussions, debates, accusations, the escape of the suspect – who is, of course, a Spartacist – and the arrest. When they finally lead the fellow away, armed men surround him, at least one threatens him with a pistol, he has to raise his hands and clasp them on his head – it looks so terribly lovely, it makes up for the long closure of the cinemas.

And so, though Munich has now been entirely conquered, we are still very far from normal circumstances. To be sure, we had newspapers again yesterday, on May 3rd, proper, uncensored bourgeois newspapers, the first since April 7th, which is also why they published a calendar of events from the past weeks, but so far they have only been local papers because we still have no way to send or receive mail, we don't know what's happening outside, we can't send word of precisely how we are faring, and both things make for an equally distressing feeling, they erase one from present-day life.

We still see no real sign of an approach to political progress after the bloody catastrophe. The old-new government merely strives to impress upon the people that it was not "White Guards" (and not "Prussians" as such, they would do well to add!) that had defeated the Spartacists, but rather "socialist troops of the socialist government" that had come to bring freedom and order. With all of the terminological confusion prevalent here, they cannot emphasize this often and firmly enough. Because the defeated party is working with the crudest of rumors and assumptions. It was said, and widely believed, that the Council Republic had been proclaimed "throughout Germany" (on the very day Munich was conquered!), and Noske now had the support of Munich alone. The government also insists that it will "anchor" the workers' councils, but to date they have not yet said anything about forming a civil militia. And yet a civil militia is the most important thing here. Either they set one up posthaste, or we'll soon be performing another act of the soviet republic when the troops withdraw. After all, there are still so many capable minds in Schwabing, and red armbands are so easy to come by. Bravo, my Munich. It should call itself Little Petersburg.

Evening. The Fatherland has definitely been saved: all of the bourgeois parties are making a fine appeal, speaking of unity, work, and bread, and rallying behind Hoffmann's government. Could one ask for any greater deeds? In addition, now that it is no longer forbidden, Epp's Freikorps is calling for recruits and seems to be targeting academics in particular. It was recently said that Bavaria's universities would be closed in order to give the students the opportunity to serve in the military. The lost semester would then be credited to them. I cannot say I find this fair, and it has provoked a sense of bitterness among a great many students – very and indeed passionately patriotic students, incidentally. For years, the students have been the ones to suffer over and over again; what good does it do them to be "credited" for all the semesters during which their studies are suspended? There is so much talk about the fair distribution of state burdens – where is the fairness here? Even a Freikorps Wolf from Swabia has posted a recruitment notice. In addition to mobilization pay, it offers a daily allowance of 10 marks and provides for mutual termination with eight days' notice. Then there is a poster from the Bavarian Supreme Commander Möhl, who thanks the northern German troops and warns the upstanding population not to give in to incitement against the Prussians; it was not true that the Prussians were consuming Munich's food, since they had brought their own provisions with them. I should state that, almost without exception, the public is indignant when it hears of attempts to stir up opinion against the Prussians; I hear many a "for shame!" All the same: when an armored vehicle with the black-and-white flag and the white death's heads of the Potsdam hussars drives down Ludwigstrasse, the people quietly watch it pass; but when the Württemberg dragoons brandish their black-and-red pennant, many, many handkerchiefs are waved... People everywhere in the city were on their feet throughout the warm spring day. Once again there was so much to see, almost more than yesterday, because the troops still continue to stream in. Music and a small parade on Ludwigstrasse and at the Field Marshals' Hall, a battery decorated by the people on the street, soldiers polishing their rifles in the gateway... A scene on Goetheplatz was particularly characteristic. A menacing cannon stood there. Across from it a stately unit marched in, cavalry, infantry, artillery. And from another street, a strange funeral procession slowly converged on the same square: two trucks, machine guns front and back, coffins in between, flowers on top and on the sides of the vehicle, the Württemberg flag out in front, and soldiers scattered everywhere in between, some of them with primed rifles. The crowd that had just been loudly cheering the incoming troops now turned silently toward the armed hearse and doffed their hats. The guards by the cannon paid none of this any heed and stood calmly by their gun. . .

A friend just phoned to tell me that he is going to Augsburg to join the Freikorps Wolf. I'll give him these pages to take.

A.B.

May 10, 1919

Outwardly Munich now makes a festive impression, one that actually gets more festive by the day. The unsettling sight of vehicles with machine guns, with trailing artillery, with soldiers perched on the radiators at the front, ready to fire, or on their stomachs on the hood, thrusting out their gun barrels or pistols, even the lone armed civilians have disappeared from the city streets, and in the evenings there is only the peaceful crack of gunshots, as in the time of the pheasant hunts under the soviet republic, without accompanying machine-gun or cannon fire. We are also allowed to be on the streets until eleven o'clock again, we are not searched as often and no longer stumble across machine guns everywhere. Instead, we have the pleasure of an abundance of proper, upright military men and jolly military music during the day, and the public never tires of watching and listening and running alongside, white handkerchiefs waving frenetically. We have a heavy cavalry unit whose buglers all sit on very white horses, and we have a volunteer corps from the uplands, the Freikorps Werdenfels as it says on its white-and-blue flag, only the smallest portion of which wears uniforms or urban civilian clothing; most of its members wear rustic, knee-length leather mountain garb, and all of them have felt Alpine hats and knapsacks, and sprays of flowers on their chests, hats, and the barrels of their guns. But above all we have Epp's corps, with the roaring golden lion's head in the black diamond on their upper arms, and the white stripes or bands around their caps and steel helmets.

And yet, Munich is not in a

festive mood, there is only concern and depression on the one side, terrible acrimony on the other. The fight was all too furious, and the desperate resistance of the communists surpassed all expectations. Even today in the bourgeois papers, next to the death notice for the widow of the land consolidation surveyor, whom no abolition of titles can abolish, we read about the death of the lieutenant who fell as a "gun commander on Lenbachplatz," the death of the "brave comrades whom our company lost in the battle for Giesing," the death of young people, bystanders who were hit on the street or in their homes, etc. etc. And how vanishingly few are identified in this way. Munich is five or six times smaller than Greater Berlin, but it has seen at least as much blood flow.[203] And time and again there were assassinations, treacherous shootings and stabbings of sentries, women and mothers were seized while holding shotguns in their hands or cranking machine guns, and then the government troops went into a frenzy as well. The dreadful shooting of 21 harmless Catholic journeymen[204] is a particularly abominable case – but who could tally up how often the terribly agitated troops used martial law[205] against individuals when, in calmer moments, even a court martial would have avoided the death penalty? It is the old, grim necessity of nature: unimpeded by a feeble government – and feeble is the mildest of epithets – the Spartacists were allowed to sow death, and now they have reaped it a hundred times over. We now have circles of people here whose grinding hatred for "bourgeoisie" and "Whites" is boundless.

And for heaven's sake, make no mistake: these circles are neither small nor unarmed nor discouraged. For a start, of the 100,000 guns distributed by the commune, fifteen thousand (according to optimistic estimates) or only five thousand (according to what are probably more precise ones) have been turned in again. So the Spartacists here have a simple and infallible means of recruiting new supporters: "Prussian" is the magic word. The Prussians waded through our blood, the Prussians are tyrannizing us, eating our bread and our fat! No denial will change this, no appeal to the level-headed citizenry to thank the Prussians as altruistic liberators, to view them simply as part of the government army, which also includes Württembergers and Bavarians – the workers and many of the little people, who forget their sorrows as quickly as they forget their joys, know what they should think of the Prussians. And they tell themselves, quite rightly, that eventually these Prussians will have to leave. How characteristic it was of the bourgeois papers to refer constantly to the fact that it was Bavarian soldiers, eight Bavarian soldiers, who murdered those poor journeymen. But how much good will this have done? No, northern German contingents will not be allowed to linger here overly long.

And what will happen when the Prussians withdraw in three or four weeks, when the de facto military dictatorship here comes to an end? I once effortlessly prophesized for you: Landauer – the poor, only half-guilty fool who had feared arrest in the last days of the commune under Levien and who has now paid with his life, while that great criminal Levien appears to have escaped, just like Toller, incidentally[206] – Landauer followed by Levien, Levien followed by Epp. I do not know the fourth man, but this cannot be stressed often or earnestly enough: he must not be named Hoffmann or else there will be a catastrophe the like of which Munich, for all of the recent atrocities, has never seen before. Hoffmann has lost to the Left and the Right; the way he still sits in Bamberg creates an impression of helplessness here, and the way the Majority Socialists are already squirming and maneuvering again creates the most embarrassing impression. For a moment it looked as though the Munich *Post* had finally, finally seen the light. On May 5th it wrote: "A new age has dawned: The people have turned their backs on the old militarism. But present circumstances do not permit the military to be abolished. Anyone who is not mentally or physically blind must have realized this in the last weeks at the latest." But a few days later it wavered again and grew very inclined to stay the hand of military force.

Of course, they have certainly not yet managed to do

this. Nonetheless, one already senses delicate half-measures in the actions of the pure socialist government. What will happen with the Munich civil militia? The "guard regiment" that is supposed to be established, a police force, cannot manage alone, and it seems that strange things are intended for the planned "residents militia." They want to store their weapons in depots, depots that everyone, including the Spartacists, will know about! A brilliant idea. By contrast, recruitment for the regular military (this is probably what we have to call the Freikorps now) is proceeding at a truly feverish pace. I sometimes have the impression that the military high command wants to squeeze as much out of Munich as possible in this regard for as long as it can; that is, as long as Hoffmann's government is not yet ruling Munich again autocratically – and impotently! Hoffmann's government, which has already had to ban recruitment here once, a scandal that could be repeated, whereupon the bourgeoisie will then stand more or less defenseless before the guns that will unquestionably appear

again in the hands of Spartacists driven mad with rancor. After all, how long will the Freikorps stay concentrated in the capital? How long will they stay together at all once Hoffmann rules "pacified" Munich once more?

You may laugh at me now if you want. Troops upon troops in Munich, and new ones continue to stream in with all of their munitions, whole baggage trains roll down Ludwigstrasse, and I have even seen machine guns on flag-bedecked children's wagons. And recruiting office upon recruiting office, and all of them flourishing. It has happened, of course, that notorious Red Guards have reported to the "Whites," only to be found out afterward. They entered into new service without malice, just as one went from the Swedish forces to Wallenstein's. The epicenter of all recruitment, the surest element to guarantee crack troops, is the university. Today it celebrated a day of honor in the very same main auditorium that had seen such splendid things during those splendid weeks. It thanked the brave prorector Friedrich von Müller, who had preserved the honor of the university under continual threat to his own life, and under whose leadership the entire faculty had remained steadfast (something that cannot be said of the technical college). It thanked the students who had already fought for Munich's liberation. But above all, it recruited – recruited passionately, ardently, and pleadingly for Epp's corps, which calls itself the "Bavarian rifle corps" and will be part of the Reichswehr. In particular, there was a young student whom I had once heard pledge loyalty to the professors in the name of his fellow students when he was a civilian, and who now wore the Iron Cross First Class and a silver Wound Badge on a simple gunner's jacket. He talked about the atmosphere in the Ohrdruf camp, about the march on Munich, about entire companies and batteries made up *solely* of officers, officers who perform rank-and-file duties and who salute like the rank and file, who want to set an example and create an "officers' reserve." There was more than just the misery of Munich behind his words, there was the entire German plight, and there was a tone to everything

he said that occasionally made me fear he might misspeak and, instead of Epp, say – Schill.[207] But we not only heard rousing speeches, we also heard precisely how the senate, in joint consultation with Colonel Epp himself, had made it possible for the students to remain dedicated to their studies while serving the Fatherland's cause at the same time. The summer semester is not supposed to start until June 16th and will be extended into the autumn accordingly. The students are supposed to enlist with the active corps for just one month and then move to the reserves, which will only be called up in emergencies (but to be clear: not just Munich emergencies, not just Bavarian emergencies!). –

This dreadfully serious assembly was not lacking in a comical intermezzo. We learned how the revolutionary university council (our friend Strasser and an equally seasoned schoolfellow, Hausdorf)[208] had come to the end of its role. The gentlemen had lastly threatened to arrest the refractory senate, which continued to work despite having been dismissed; threatening the use of armed force, they had compelled the senate to hand over the keys to the dean's office. On May 1st, the heroes disappeared. In their place, a small, frightened girl appeared before a professor. One of the tyrants had given the keys to his sister to deliver, and she had entrusted them to a friend, and the friend, in turn, had gotten scared and, in her fear, threw the keys into the Isar River, and now she wanted to confess everything. . .

The audience laughed heartily, but it was only a brief moment of mirth. Then seriousness was once again given its bitter due. Except that none of these young men, for all of their seriousness, had any fears any longer, either for Munich itself or regarding the Spartacists. On this point they are certain of victory. I myself am not. A man, and not a Hoffmann, must lead us, and the bourgeoisie must lend him manly support – or is that really so impossible? This is the only way things will go well for Munich. Otherwise – I recommend that northern Germans not take a summer trip to Munich or the Bavarian uplands. You may remember a much-ridiculed saying from the *ancien régime*: A warning to the curious![209]

A.B.

There was heavy fire in the inner city: rifle fire, machine-gun fire, grenades, mines – the Spartacists could not have been completely annihilated yet, as a skirmish, a veritable battle, was under way. It couldn't last long; an entire army was moving in, after all, new troops marching all the time, and the Spartacists would certainly be strangled in a few hours. But the battle lasted throughout the night and for the whole of the following day. And even once every part of Munich was undoubtedly in the hands of Reich troops, the fighting still did not stop, not for days. You awoke to the blast of a few hand grenades, followed by gunfire, then the artillery joined in, and an hour would pass before peace returned. You walked down a quiet street – and suddenly a shout from somewhere: "Clear the street, there's about to be shooting!", and before you had even reached the entrance to a house, the whistles and bangs would start; you opened a window, something whizzed past your ear, and you immediately saw two lines of soldiers pressed against the walls of the houses, moving down the street, each aiming a primed rifle at the windows on the other side. At first it was said: "The Spartacists are defending themselves out of pure desperation because they know they've lost – after murdering the hostages, they can't expect any pardon." But anyone who survived the actual days of combat would have had the opportunity to flee or hide – so why the continued wild assaults on guards and patrols, for which the attackers always ultimately paid with their lives? It was not merely desperation, it was boundless rancor, it was an unquestioning heroism that compelled these people to keep fighting. Where did my sympathies lie? Certainly not with the Spartacists.

Their political principle amounted to serfdom, and their behavior in Munich had long been childish before ultimately tipping over into bloody fanaticism. But even the victorious troops – and with such a superior force, victory was hardly a heroic feat – displayed little by way of humanity. Granted, they were provoked to the extreme by the murder of the hostages, by the unexpectedly fierce resistance, and afterward by the repeated and often treacherous flare-ups of an opposition thought to have been extinguished. But how many atrocities they committed. The case of the Catholic journeymen's association caused the greatest stir. Twenty-one piously Catholic, respectably bourgeois journeymen sat together peacefully and were shot by mistake, so to speak, by an invading patrol that took them for communists before they could identify themselves. The Munich papers heavily emphasized that the tragic error had befallen Bavarian, not Prussian, soldiers. At the same time, posters insisted that the Berlin Guards Riflemen were not living off of Munich's supplies but had instead brought their own provisions with them. Both of these publications were necessary, because sympathy for the Prussian liberators had already dried up, no one waved handkerchiefs at them anymore, and they were insulted behind their backs. If the Red and White fighters held little appeal for me, the citizens of Munich were more repellent to me than ever. I stood among them on the second day of fighting, on the

Stachus square one moment, at the Propylaea gate the next. This was the edge of the combat zone, where the blockades began, where new troops went into battle, and from time to time a grenade howled close by. Then everyone would scurry back, hole up in the entrance of a house – and emerge again two minutes later. The Stachus had a wildly romantic look about it. In the middle of the square a little shop had been gutted by fire and the advertising pillars next to it shattered by a grenade; the roof beams of the big Mathäser building were destroyed, the gray houses bore the traces of numerous bullets, a hole had been shot in the cupola of the Palace of Justice, the square tower of the Protestant church bore wounds (my wife had unwittingly played on in there as the fighting began). And there were bullet-riddled windows and the ragged snarl of dangling wires everywhere. And machine guns everywhere, the long bullet belt inserted and ready for use, and everywhere there were guards, patrols, and larger formations. The public did not limit itself to observation and discussion, it wanted to play along and fell back on the same game over and over again. Every once in a while someone aroused suspicion. He was supposed to have expressed sympathy with the Reds – instead of "Reds" they also liked to say "Jewish pigs" – he was supposed to have been wearing a remarkably new white armband – "it was probably a red one yesterday" – he was supposed to have been "seen with one," supposed to own a Spartacus book. Then he would be surrounded, threatened with a pistol by at least one person, he had to put his hands over his head and was pushed and shoved to the nearest patrol. Where did my sympathies lie? Still with the academics, more than anyone. In the main auditorium there was a victory meeting that simultaneously turned into a recruiting event for Epp's Freikorps. Recruiting offices for the Freikorps, previously prohibited in Munich, had now opened up everywhere. But Epp's "rifle corps" was particularly dependent on students and was swathed in a special academic glory. Its leader – decorated as a young colonial officer at the start of the century, and the first bourgeois commander of the Lifeguards during the world war – was considered by the university to be the actual savior and actual future hope of the poor Fatherland. Epp had entire companies consisting of nothing but students, students who had been lieutenants in the war and now performed rank-and-file duties. One of these young men gave the victory and recruitment speech. In my account of it, I wrote a sentence I was proud of: "I was always afraid he would misspeak and instead of Epp say: Schill." But I harbored another fear as well, one which I kept to myself, in this article anyway. When the zealous speaker mentioned the "foreign elements" against whom the Fatherland would have to be protected in the future, I was always afraid that instead of "foreign elements" he would say "Jewish pigs." And at the same time I heard the accusation of Rabinowitz: "You're playing the Protestant." No, I wasn't playing the Protestant. I was Protestant, because I was German. But would this lot acknowledge that, my Germanness? Did I have to conceal my heritage? My heart had grown very heavy. The university established a formal alliance with Epp. The summer semester would be organized so that the students could serve for a few days and study for a few days – and later, as I said, those who had never taken the matriculation exam would be exempted from it as long as they joined the Freikorps. The lecturers themselves were supposed to set a good example and receive military training in the corps for a while, and the corps solemnly swore that they would be treated with the utmost respect during drills, and that their academic work would be respected as well. Anyone who had fought in the war need not even go to the barracks; a signature was enough to join Epp's emergency reserves, which would only be called up in cases of urgent need. I signed such a pledge as well. I do not know what became of my Spartacus Lieutenant Strasser, or whether he has some connection to the Strasser of the National Socialists, but I do know that my Colonel Epp became a governor in the Third Reich.[210] Several weeks after this recruitment assembly, I entered the university towards evening through the back entrance on Amalienstrasse. We now had our own security force since there was unrest all over the state and it could have broken out again any day in Munich. Someone shouted at me from fairly far away – "Stop, are you authorized?" – and he swung his rifle from his shoulder rather wildly and approached me. We recognized each other at the same moment. "Pardon me, friend . . ." – "Oh, it's you, Matthias Meier.[211] I had no idea you were so martial." The little man under the steel helmet was generally referred to as Galimathias Meier by us lecturers; he had habilitated in Catholic philosophy under Baeumker and was a very peaceable person and very pleasant colleague. Politically he belonged to the left wing of the Center Party and approved of the Weimar Coalition[212] just as much as I did. "I couldn't get out of it," he said. "You signed too, after all – but you have it easier – I have to drill and stand guard." – "Is the safety engaged on your rifle?" – "No, how do you do that?" I cautiously stepped behind him and engaged the safety. "There could be an accident otherwise if you swing that rifle around so boldly." – "I know," he said, "I shot the ceiling earlier. But nothing happened." He musingly added, "Say, who are we actually serving with Epp? Is it really the republic and peace?" "It's the lesser evil, in any case," I said. I was pleased with my answer, but I was not very much at ease.

Although he was doing badly, Hans Meyerhof, in his mixture of obstinacy and playfulness, was generally better off than I was at the time; he felt no conflict within himself, he relished the adventure of the situation – ten years later I would learn just how much.[213] A lucky accident protected him during the days of fighting. At the end of April he had given himself a hernia that required immediate surgery. On May 4th I visited him in the villa-like Israelite hospital out on the Bavariaring. Manhunts and house searches were taking place all over the city; it was said that captured Bavarian soldiers still had a strange inclination to make escape attempts resulting in death, just as they had during the war outside. I found Hans in a small two-bed room; the other bed was unoccupied. He appeared to be without pain, but he was still weak and very pale; his face looked nearly green in the frame of his heavy red beard. At the head of his bed, hardly any less pale than he was, stood his evil demon Weckerle, recounting the murderous deeds of the Whites. He himself had managed to avoid arrest thus far, but he had not yet succeeded in leaving Munich. When he saw me, he very abruptly ended his report. "I'll leave you to your bourgeois friend," he concluded hostilely and left without shaking my hand. Standing in the doorway, he added: "The Council Republic is coming. If it is stifled here, it will rise up somewhere else." I did not see him again and only heard later from Hans that he had escaped and was working somewhere in the west, Darmstadt I believe, for a communist newspaper. "Hans," I said as soon as Weckerle was gone from the room, "let's not get political right now – do you have dangerous papers with you?" – "My briefcase is here in the nightstand, there's nothing else." – "That's just enough, Hans." The wallet held his membership card for the Spartacus League and his authorization to make arrests. I took both papers out and flushed them down the nearest lavatory. Afterwards I advised him: "If they interrogate you, mention me, you can say I'm the correspondent for the *Leipziger Neueste Nachrichten*, but you don't have to think me a traitor for that, I always stressed Eisner's and Landauer's pure idealism, and I opposed the anti-Semitism of the citizens and the students." I said that to appease Hans, because I thought he would vehemently attack me. Yet he just laughed, not even mockingly, but rather with a kind of appreciation. Sending dispatches practically from the headquarters of the Council Republic to a Pan-German paper while there was talk of "foreign letters" being monitored – that was risky and adventurous, too, after all. Two hours after my visit, the police checked Hans's jacket pockets and wallet. I heard about it the next day from Hamecher, who had himself ensured that nothing incriminating was found in the smuggler's den. The military had searched it, Elena had been arrested but released again soon after, she had played dumb, and her deafness had stood her in very good stead. Hamecher also reported that the people had a list of everyone who associated with Meyerhof. "Your name was on it." That was fine, I said, I had told Hans that he should mention me as a witness; but inwardly I was unsettled.

Munich Tragicomedy

[January 17, 1920]

People in more robust times have known both tragedy and comedy, have allowed their hearts to convulse with heroic suffering and their bellies to shake with clownish behavior. But the fact that a fate can be doubly tragic, in that it devolves into the pathetically absurd, is something only modern man has realized, and a sense of tragicomedy is virtually a defining characteristic of recent epochs. In scholarly terms, this difficult concept of tragicomedy is still contested – so it could certainly do no harm to provide a few examples of it from real life. It seems to me that Bavaria's public life is currently no more lacking in this regard than its libraries are lacking precious manuscripts.

A peculiar collection of books has been up for sale here for quite some time. It is modest and not to be found in any of the large antiquarian bookshops, but rather stacked in chaotic and dusty piles in the humble room of a small dealer. The expert can see at a glance what he is dealing with: it is the library of a journalist who had more interests than money. Most of the more expensive books are paperbound and stamped with "Review Copy," and they come from the most varied domains, history and politics, *belles-lettres*, art, erotic literature. The books purchased by the owner himself pertain mostly to philosophy, literature, aesthetics. The owner occasionally spent good money on philosophical works. I take him to be a columnist with a good education who occasionally (but only rarely) crossed over into politics. Or perhaps he also had a philological streak? Professional interest compels me to reach for a book with the title *Abrégé de la syntaxe française*, Lindauer Publishers, Munich, 1912. I open the volume – it contains an anti-militaristic and Bolshevist leaflet printed in Zurich in 1916. Smuggled in and – at least at the time – treasonous, murderous agitational material. All of these books bear the stamp and sometimes the handwritten name of their owner: *Kurt Eisner*. You can tell a man by his library. A man's profession can usually also be determined by his collection of books. But who would have guessed this was the library of a Bavarian prime minister? This is Munich tragicomedy.

The man whose political education is revealed by his library, and whose beneficial activity for the welfare of Bavaria and Germany aligns with this political education, is shot by an overheated patriot, and Eisner's death brings almost more disaster upon us than his life. From February to May 1919, Munich in particular cannot escape the tragicomedy.

Everything is wretched, and everything is bloody, and you always want to laugh and cry at once.

Then the situation is "brought to order" (or what they call "order"), and we can almost believe that we have a proper government. It was in Bamberg, of course, since circumstances had grown precarious here, but at last it gradually, gradually dared to return to Munich.

It was not until yesterday, January 16th, after a months-long pause, that things looked somewhat more critical again in Munich. The trial of Eisner's assassin, Arco, who now appears to be a martyr to many, just as Eisner once appeared to be a martyr to many. (In terms of the political maturity of the prime minister and his assassin, incidentally, one was as bad as the other.) The court plays at being Brutus. Fervent patriotism and an example for the youth are acknowledged (by the prosecutor!) and confirmed in the sentence, but it is a death sentence. Quite nice on stage ("My cousin Friedrich wants to play at being Brutus"[214] – Hohenzollern, by the way, not Ebert), but in life? What an abundance of tragicomedy here, too, especially when one considers that this "people's court" has underscored the patriotism and honor of the man who shot the founder of the Free State of Bavaria!

Once the death sentence has been pronounced, the tragicomedy continues in earnest. The students demonstrate. Arco, who certainly must be viewed and pitied in human terms, suddenly becomes their hero. In the evening they file down Ludwigstrasse in close formation, several hundred strong. They sing "Watch on the Rhine" – and forget that the Rhine is currently being held by black French troops, they sing "Deutschland über alles" and have no better cause to do so than a political murder. They pass by the Ministry of War, where the sentries with steel helmets and hand grenades (often in white Carpathian fur) are already a familiar sight and no longer even attract attention, and the sentries, who are supposed to remain neutral toward demonstrators as long as there is no need for defense – they wave their arms and helmets jubilantly.

As the gesture of just a few people who were probably students themselves, this is barely given any notice. The next day, however, it appears that it heralded a pinnacle of Munich tragicomedy. From ten-thirty on, students crowd into the main auditorium by the hundreds, or more likely by the thousands, because once again, as in those feverish spring days of the previous year, the windows have been removed, and the corridors open onto the giant, overcrowded lecture hall. Only a rustling is heard from the crowd, in which the green, red and blue caps of the fraternities form colorful and not especially large islands. There is no talking, only waiting. Mutely and imposingly. The street and building complex have been occupied by the military, but all is calm outside as well. From time to time Rector Müller appears, or the rector of the technical college, von Dyck[215] (the students from the college have convened in a special room), and he asks briefly for continued patience. The council of ministers is in session, and the result of the meeting will be announced here shortly. And finally, at ten-thirty, the result: Count Arco's sentence has been commuted to life imprisonment. A clamor, caps and arms thrown aloft, greater rejoicing than has ever greeted a German victory. And then the loveliest thing. My fellow students, a student representative says, let us thank the Reichswehr! Yesterday its local Group Command declared solidarity with our demand that Count Arco be pardoned! More and louder cheering. And they don't realize what it is they're celebrating: troops who dictate to the government how it should behave, who obey only conditionally.

And if only it were just the young, enthusiastic students who did not realize this. But I would bet this much: our Hoffmann government will surely also not realize it, and will remain in office as before, and will continue to call itself a "government" as before. And Herr Hoffmann has good reason not to notice anything: he has left the city again, as he always does when he begins to feel slightly uneasy in Munich.

After all of this, I would like to be so bold as to offer my own definition of tragicomedy: it is tragic for the person involved and comical for the indifferent bystander. What a pity that one cannot simultaneously be a mere bystander when one is German.

A.B.

Appendix

The first page of the manuscript of Klemperer's "Revolutionary Diary" from 1919.

The German Revolution of 1918–19

A historical essay

Wolfram Wette

Even 100 years later, the German revolution of 1918–19 attracts our interest. This should come as no surprise. It was the only revolution to have taken place in Germany to that point, and it was relatively successful. It produced the first German democracy, the Weimar Republic. The revolution of 1918–19 was a turning point in modern German history. It has a permanent place in Germany's memory of its democratic traditions. To understand the reasons for this revolution and the forms that it took, it is important to know that it was nothing less than a strategically planned coup by professional revolutionaries who were prepared to use violence. No, it was born from the protest of millions of Germans against the Great War, which had lasted for four years. The war had brought death and misery to the country, and most people longed for a swift end to it. From 1916 the country was ruled by a military dictatorship, namely, the Supreme Army Command (*Oberste Heeresleitung*, or OHL) under General Field Marshal Paul von Hindenburg and his deputy, General Erich Ludendorff. The latter was the actual strongman in the OHL.

In the spring and summer of 1918, it became apparent that these generals were still making no effort to move toward a "negotiated peace." A parliamentary majority had proposed this as a political goal one year earlier. Instead, those in power wanted to continue fighting and let the "homeland" continue suffering in order to achieve the military "victorious peace" that was supposedly still possible. This was the breeding ground for the protest movements that emerged in the course of 1918, both on the front line and back at home. In March, German soldiers on the Western front, on French soil, made their feelings about Germany's war policy known by engaging in a "covert military strike" that they concealed from the military leadership. Major strikes were held at home as well, even in armaments plants critical to the war effort. A massive anti-war movement formed and took to the streets demanding "Peace, Freedom, Bread!" – "peace" meaning a rapid end to the war, "freedom" meaning replacing the militaristic authoritarian state with a democratic republic, and "bread" meaning the state should focus at long last on feeding its needy population, in part by endeavoring to lift the Allied blockade on food imports.

At the end of October and start of November 1918, sailors from the Imperial High Seas Fleet mutinied, first in Wilhelmshaven and then in Kiel, in the hopes of quickly ending the war. By fundamentally calling the old power structures into question while simultaneously allying themselves with the local workforce, the sailors gave the signal for the start of the German revolution. This spread like a tidal wave from the north to cover all of Germany. It arrived in Munich on November 7 and 8, 1918, even before it had reached the imperial capital of Berlin. As had previously happened in Kiel, revolutionary soldiers allied themselves with revolutionary workers in many other German cities. From their own ranks they appointed workers' and soldiers' councils on a local, regional, and national level, and these revolutionary ruling bodies took the place of the old powers.

A politically decisive breakthrough was achieved on November 9 in Berlin. The workers in Berlin's large factories went on general strike. The soldiers in the garrison declared their solidarity with the strikers. Under pressure, Kaiser Wilhelm II abdicated. Reich Chancellor Prince Max von Baden relinquished his office to the chairman of the Majority Social Democratic Party of Germany (MSPD), Friedrich Ebert. Philipp Scheidemann, a long-serving parliamentarian and one of the best-known members of the MSPD, proclaimed from the balcony of the Reichstag building: "Long live the German Republic!" A few streets away, Reichstag delegate Karl Liebknecht from the Independent Social

Democratic Party of Germany (USPD) proclaimed the "Free Socialist Republic of Germany."

Then came the revolution "from below." Under pressure from the rank and file, who were pushing for the two social democratic parties to join forces, a new government was brought into being on November 10, 1918, a revolutionary body calling itself the Council of People's Deputies. It was made up of three experienced politicians each from the two social democratic parties. Ebert assumed chairmanship of it. This revolutionary government issued an important proclamation on November 12, 1918, *"An das deutsche Volk!"* ("To the German People!"), in which it announced the enforcement of political reforms: the introduction of an eight-hour workday as well as general, equal, secret, and direct voting rights for everyone from the age of 20 (including women), and the election of a constituent National Assembly. The issue of socialization – that is, the communization of the means of production – was not addressed in the proclamation. This was due to the two parties' differing ideas about the goals of the revolution, and it would be a source of conflict in the following months. The revolutionary upheaval in the Reich capital of Berlin, which would affect the entire German Reich, was largely calm and bloodless – contrary to some expectations. The old system collapsed without a fight. Some historians believe the peaceful course of the November Revolution can be attributed to the fact that the old powers resigned without resistance. Others point out the country's advanced state of democratization and high degree of industrialization and, as a result of these two factors, the German population's widespread anti-chaos instinct, which included a desire for administrative continuity.

On November 11, 1918, the guns finally fell silent, just as the mass movement had been demanding for months. But the leading generals Hindenburg and Ludendorff evaded having to sign the armistice and thus accept responsibility for the military defeat of the German Reich. Instead, the government of People's Deputies sent Center Party politician Matthias Erzberger to the French city of Compiègne to sign the armistice agreement. In the period that followed, the responsible officers led millions of German soldiers from the front lines back to Germany, where they were demobilized. Spontaneous demobilizations occurred wherever the military bureaucracy was unable to issue proper discharge papers. Everyone was happy to have survived the war, and they all desperately wanted to be back home before Christmas.

While the revolutionary upheaval was under way in Berlin, German NCO Victor Klemperer was in the Lithuanian city of Vilnius, which was occupied by German troops. In 1915, the 34-year-old (born October 9, 1881) – who was married and had both a doctorate and a university lecturer's qualification in Romance philology – had reported as a war volunteer as proof of his patriotism. Klemperer, the son of a Jewish father and Jewish mother, also demonstrated his eagerness to assimilate by converting to Protestantism. From November 1915 to March 1916 he was deployed on the Western front, in Flanders. In the autumn of 1918 he was performing relatively safe military duties in Vilnius, in the press office of the staff of *Ober Ost*, as the office of the supreme commander of the entire German armed forces in the East was known.

After the armistice agreement of Compiègne, Klemperer swiftly found a way to get back to the West entirely legally by train. He first stopped over for several weeks in Leipzig, where his wife, Eva, lived, and then traveled on in mid-December 1918 to spend a few days in Munich, where his reserve unit, the "Prince Luitpold" 7th Field Artillery Regiment, was stationed. Sergeant Klemperer placed great value in bringing his military service to a formally proper end. His former regimental comrades honored this by not only issuing him the necessary discharge papers without complaint, but also furnishing him with wages, leave and ration cards.

On December 16, 1918, the National Congress of Workers' and Soldiers' Councils convened in Berlin, where it would spend many days setting the course for Germany's political future. It became apparent that the majority of workers' and soldiers' councils followed the moderate line of the Majority Social Democrats. The National Congress called for the "demolition of militarism," by which it meant, first and foremost, the disempowerment of the career officers who had been socially dominant and politically influential in the German Empire. It additionally rejected the introduction of a "pure councils system" as an alternative to a parliamentary system of government, and it endorsed elections to the National Assembly, which were scheduled for January 19, 1919. Differing opinions on questions of military policy led the representatives of the Independent Social Democrats to leave the government of People's Deputies at the end of December 1918. They were replaced by Majority Social Democratic politicians. Responsibility for the army and navy was handed to Reichstag member Gustav Noske.

Even in January 1919, Noske dealt very harshly with demonstrators in the capital who were not satisfied with the course of the revolution thus far and were prepared to take up arms in order to push it further. Noske deployed the military to quash the January unrest in Berlin, which even the propaganda at the time erroneously referred to as a "Spartacist uprising." A police-based solution to the problem was not seriously considered or thought to be possible, either at that time or during later disturbances. What resulted were clashes resembling a civil war. They began in January 1919 in Berlin and, over the following months, moved to Bremen, then back to Berlin (March Fighting of 1919), the Ruhr region, Braunschweig, Magdeburg, the Eastern provinces, Württemberg, and finally, in May 1919, Munich. This civil war claimed the lives of around 3,000 people.

The consistent characteristic of these inner-societal conflicts in the first half of 1919 was that any attempt at revolutionary change beyond the democratization of Germany as agreed by the National Congress of Councils was stifled by the government of People's Deputies using military force. One tool of this national policy of violence was the Freikorps, or volunteer paramilitary units, the creation of which had been called for by Noske in January 1919. Most of the men who heeded this call were former career soldiers with anti-democratic and counter-revolutionary leanings who bristled at the prospect of having to join the civilian working world. The violent suppression of the councils' experiments in different parts of Germany – without having previously explored options for negotiation or de-escalation – was the negative hallmark of the "Noske era." This policy of violence was based on the dubious claim that Germany had to be protected against "Bolshevism." It was not by chance that Reichswehr soldiers referred to this phase, during which the second wave of revolution was violently crushed, as the "after-war," making it clear that they felt the external war was now being continued within Germany. The National Assembly elections on January 19, 1919, resulted in a majority for an alliance made up of the Majority Social Democratic Party, the Catholic Center Party and the German Democratic Party (DDP). This alliance was known as the Weimar Coalition. Its delegates elected Friedrich Ebert, a Social Democrat and former chairman of the government of People's Deputies, as the first President of the Republic. Ebert gave Philipp Scheidemann the task of forming a government. Scheidemann became the first Chancellor of the Republic in the government that was formed on February 13, 1919. In the first half of 1919, a commission chaired by the constitutional law expert Hugo Preuss produced a draft of the Weimar Constitution. It was adopted on July 31, 1919, by the National Assembly in Weimar.

The Treaty of Versailles, which had been drawn up by the Allied powers without the involvement of the Germans, was fiercely rejected by the German government and most members of the National Assembly, who referred to it as a "diktat." On May 12, 1919, in the National Assembly in Berlin, Philipp Scheidemann exclaimed: "Which hand would not wither, having placed itself and us in such shackles?" After rejecting the treaty in such terms, he was forced to resign as the head of government when it became clear that no change was possible. Against the protest of parties on the Right, a majority of the National Assembly (257 to 138 votes) ultimately accepted the terms of the peace treaty. Even the oppositional Independent Social Democrats agreed to it.

*

This is the wider historical background to the regional political events that Victor Klemperer personally experienced in Munich. He recorded the activities and his impressions of them in a "Revolutionary Diary" and reported on them for the *Leipziger Neueste Nachrichten*, a conservative, counter-revolutionary newspaper. Once he had arranged for his proper discharge from military service in mid-December 1918, he prepared to return to civilian professional life, which meant resuming his job as a university lecturer for modern French literature at Ludwig-Maximilian University in Munich. In light of the acute housing shortage, it proved very difficult to find suitable lodgings for himself and his wife. The Klemperers spent the Christmas holidays of 1918 and January 1919 in Leipzig, and at the end of the month they both moved to Munich, where Klemperer's wife planned to continue her organ studies. They initially lived in a boarding house. Since Klemperer did not receive a regular salary as a lecturer, he was dependent on financial support from his brothers during this transitional period.

Klemperer had actually wanted to focus entirely on his private affairs in 1919. But in this time of revolutionary upheaval, politics continually intruded on his life, whether he wanted them to or not. He had already encountered workers' and soldiers' councils in Leipzig, and he had little sympathy for them. In contrast to the relatively calm situation in Leipzig, he found Munich in early February 1919 to be a city in a state of high political agitation, though he took this to be less a precursor to violent conflict than an amusing diversion, a "political carnival" with many colorful flags and pennants. He wondered what Munich was actually celebrating: the end of the war, or the victory of the revolution?

The revolution had already claimed victory here on November 7, 1918. On the night of November 7, at a meeting of the Munich Workers' and Soldiers' Council, the USPD politician Kurt Eisner proclaimed the "Free State of Bavaria" (meaning "free" from the monarchy) and declared the abdication of Bavarian King Ludwig III – thus ending the 738-year rule of the Wittelsbach dynasty in one fell swoop. The Munich Workers' and Soldiers' Council elected Eisner as the first prime minister of the Free State. As would later happen on a national level, the Majority Social Democrats and Independents agreed to form a joint revolutionary government in Bavaria. It remained in office for a transitional period of 100 days, until Eisner was assassinated on February 21, 1919.

Kurt Eisner was a writer, journalist, and politician. He had spent many years working for the Social Democratic paper *Vorwärts* and other SPD party newspapers, where he had earned a good reputation. Soon after 1914, he began to doubt the official version of Germany's defensive warfare. It became increasingly clear to him that Germany was responsible for the war. He began to have pacifist leanings in 1915, and in 1917 he joined the newly founded Independent Social Democratic Party, which brought together the social democratic opponents of the war. He was a co-founder of the USPD in Munich and Bavaria and became the party's leading figure.

On the very day that the "Free State of Bavaria" was proclaimed, Eisner announced that he wanted to convene a constituent Bavarian assembly as soon as possible. He called upon the population to help ensure "that the inevitable change takes place quickly, easily, and peacefully." Following his pacifist convictions, he declared: "In this time of senselessly wild murder, we abhor all bloodshed. Every human life is sacred."

No profound political changes were achieved during the short Eisner era. The MSPD members of his government – like their counterparts on a national level – held the view that only a freely elected state parliament should determine the future shape of the Free State of Bavaria, and that Eisner's cabinet was merely a provisional solution. Elections to the Bavarian State Parliament were held on January 12, 1919. The SPD took 33% of the vote, while the conservative Bavarian People's Party (BVP), which had carried out an anti-Semitic defamation campaign against the "Jewish-Bolshevist revolution," won 35%. Eisner's own party, the USPD, suffered a dramatic defeat with only 2.52% of the votes.

When the newly elected Bavarian State Parliament met on February 21, 1919, Eisner set off to announce his resignation as prime minister. But he was never able to do so. On his way to the parliament building, he was shot dead by the law student and furloughed infantry lieutenant Anton Graf Arco auf Valley. His assassin came from the orbit of the populist, anti-Semitic, anti-democratic and counter-revolutionary Thule Society.

In response to the murder of their top man, the USPD called for a general strike in Munich. The Central Council of the Bavarian Republic, which had been appointed by the Bavarian councils congress, provisionally assumed governmental power. When Kurt Eisner was buried on February 26, 1919, over 100,000 people were said to have joined his funeral procession. This expression of sympathy proved once again what Klemperer had noted with astonishment weeks earlier at a campaign rally for Eisner: that this "delicate, tiny, frail, stooped little man," "whose pure will no one could deny," was celebrated by the "real" population of Munich – "workers, tradesmen, shopkeepers."

Much like the murder of the Spartacist leaders Rosa Luxemburg and Karl Liebknecht by the radical right-wing officers of the Guards Cavalry Rifle Division (GKSD) in Berlin on January 15, 1919, the assassination of the Social Democrat Kurt Eisner was a rupture in Bavaria's political development during the revolutionary transitional period. This political murder thrust Bavaria into a violent conflict between revolutionary and counter-revolutionary forces. The subsequent general strike led to a revival and radicalization of the councils movement, and thus to a rejection of Eisner's principle of non-violence. Klemperer watched disconcertedly as a good number of students and professors in his university milieu stylized the assassin Arco as a patriotic hero.

In the phase after Eisner's death, the councils movement – which had radical leftist leanings and was clearly in a minority position – vied with the elected Bavarian State Parliament for the right to form a government. On March 1, 1919, the Central Council of the councils movement elected the Social Democrat Martin Segitz as prime minister, and on March 17 the State Parliament followed suit by electing the SPD politician Johannes Hoffmann as prime minister. When it became apparent that Hoffmann's government could not withstand the pressure of the Munich councils movement, the government fled to Bamberg. In Munich, left-wing radicals proclaimed the Council

Republic on April 7, 1919. Their government was initially led by pacifist intellectuals such as Gustav Landauer, Erich Mühsam, and Ernst Toller, but they were booted out after just one week by the communists Eugen Leviné, Max Levien, and Rudolf Egelhofer, who proclaimed a second Council Republic.

This development mobilized the Reich government in Berlin. Reich Minister of Defense Noske was given the task of "cleaning up" Munich, using violence if necessary. Although Prime Minister Hoffmann hoped that a solution could be reached through negotiation, and although there were men among the radical leftist council rulers who wanted to prevent bloodshed at all costs, the Reich's intervention against the state took a course entirely in keeping with the military logic behind it. In early May 1919 a contingent of around 30,000 Freikorps soldiers, comprising troops from Prussia, Bavaria, and Württemberg, set out in the direction of Munich. Though the communist-led council government had resolved to lay down all weapons even before the government troops marched in, it was impossible to prevent the violent clash to come. Now the "white terror" of the Freikorps battled the "red terror" of the pretentiously named "Red Army." Laden with anti-Bolshevist images of their enemy, the Freikorps soldiers employed brutal violence and, as Noske put it in his memoirs of the time, were practically in a "bloodlust" as they attacked the Red Army soldiers of the Council Republic, who were "murderous Bolshevist beasts" in their eyes. In this uneven battle, between 500 and 1,000 supporters of the Council Republic are reported to have lost their lives in the first days of May 1919 – and this despite the fact that the regional council's experiment never had even the slightest chance of establishing a permanent foothold in conservative Bavaria.

Klemperer repeatedly visited the sites of violent conflict in Munich. With astonishment, he followed the fierce and heroic resistance of the supporters of the Council Republic against the far superior forces of the Reich. He noted with surprise that Munich's bourgeoisie now actually welcomed the arrival of Prussian troops. Klemperer also noticed the change in the balance of power by observing the behavior of individuals who surreptitiously switched their red armbands for white ones. But in the hottest phases of the conflict, the wider political context remained a mystery to the diarist, as no newspapers were being published in Munich that could have given him an insight into activities in the Reich.

Klemperer closely observed several key players in the councils movement and recorded his impressions in astute portraits. We get to know Kurt Eisner, Kurt Landauer, and Max Levien, but also the DDP politician Ludwig Quidde, Karl Escherich, whom Klemperer confused with Karl's brother Georg (founder of an anti-republican paramilitary organization in response to the Munich Council Republic), and the Freikorps leader Franz Ritter von Epp, who helped crush the Munich Council Republic with his force of 700 men. In each phase of events, Klemperer tried to capture the political atmosphere in Munich, which was quite peaceful for long stretches. The obvious lack of political professionalism on the part of the revolutionary protagonists and the folkloristic appearance of their supporters prompted Klemperer to repeatedly draw comparisons with a "carnival commotion" or a "farce" that had nothing serious about it.

In terms of his own political position, Klemperer remained ambivalent during this time of revolutionary upheaval. He abhorred the radical left-wing Spartacists just as much as the right-wing nationalists. He flirted instead with the moderate Right. When it came time to cast a vote for the National Assembly on January 19, 1919, Klemperer – who had voted for the SPD in the past – opted for the Liberals, or more specifically, for the German Democratic Party (DDP), which was to the left of Gustav Stresemann's German People's Party (DVP). With this vote, Klemperer wanted to support the moderate Weimar Coalition.

In his chronicle of the months of revolutionary upheaval, he also reports on everyday life at the University of Munich. His academic duties were especially challenging in these eventful times, as most of the students were former front-line soldiers who had to attend lectures during a "war emergency semester." On the one hand they had a fierce hunger for knowledge, but on the other hand they quickly lost interest if they doubted the practical use of what they were learning. When

Epp's counter-revolutionary Freikorps began recruiting volunteers, a good number of students signed up.

As a man of Jewish descent (his father was a rabbi, his mother was Jewish as well) who had converted to Protestantism, Klemperer was wide awake to the anti-Semitic tendencies apparent in the revolutionary months of 1918–19. He was not blind to the anti-Semitic attitudes directed against the revolutionaries by sections of the Munich bourgeoisie, the Bavarian People's Party, the professors, the students, and the Freikorps soldiers. Several leading figures in the Munich councils movement were indeed of Jewish descent, including the Social Democrat Kurt Eisner and the more radical politicians and writers Gustav Landauer, Max Levien, Eugen Leviné, Erich Mühsam, and Ernst Toller. But the counter-revolution was interested not in individuals, but rather in branding the key players in the Bavarian councils movements as "Jewish pigs" across the board. At the same time, they made Jews into the scapegoat for all the wrongs of the age: for inciting the world war, for the military defeat, and, ultimately, for the revolution. Klemperer was attacked from the other side as well: a fanatic Zionist once informed him that she did not associate with converted Jews, those "traitors."

Looking back, it is important to realize one thing: the German populists and nationalists who embodied the counterrevolution in 1918–19 were already turning "Jewish Bolshevism" into the bogeyman that would be used as a propagandistic backdrop to the Wehrmacht's war against the Soviet Union in 1941. An officer in the Imperial German Navy, Commander Bogislaw von Selchow, described a scene in Berlin on November 11, 1918, as follows: "In the morning I went to the Imperial Naval Office, which was flying the red flag. A Jewish Bolshevik in civilian clothing stood guard outside with a shotgun. It was all like a bad dream [. . .]." In Munich, Eisner's assassin Graf Arco auf Valley justified his deed by saying: "Eisner is a Bolshevist, he is a Jew, he is not a German, he does not feel German, he undermines every patriotic thought and feeling, he is a traitor to the nation." Klemperer was greatly concerned by the aggressive anti-Semitism he witnessed in Munich in the revolutionary year 1919. Though he did not yet feel directly threatened, he was "depressed and isolated" by it nonetheless.

*

The bloody end of the socialist councils era was followed by a counter-revolution. Conservative, reactionary, populist, and anti-Semitic forces grew stronger in Bavaria even more quickly than in other parts of the country. This was the political climate that gave birth to the Nazi Party.

In the second half of 1919, following the successful military defeat of the second revolutionary wave, the political influence of the Right and the military strengthened throughout Germany. These forces accepted neither the Weimar Republic nor the government nor the Treaty of Versailles. In particular, they bristled at the military disarmament provisions stipulated by the Versailles treaty. This development ultimately culminated in a military coup against the republic in March 1920. It was instigated by the reactionary East Prussian regional director-general Wolfgang Kapp and the highest-ranking officer in the Provisional Reichswehr, General Walther von Lüttwitz. For this reason, it is known as the Kapp-Lüttwitz Putsch.

The Reich government, led by the Social Democrat Gustav Bauer, was forced to flee from Berlin to Stuttgart. Gustav Noske, who had lost political command of the military, had to vacate his post as Reich Minister of Defense. It took a general strike proclaimed by the unions and the political parties on the Left to fend off the putsch against the republic. But the nationalist Right had shown that it would not accept the defeat in the war, the "dictated peace" of the Treaty of Versailles, the forced disarmament or the democratization of politics. The opponents of the republic were bent on restoration and revenge.

*

Klemperer, who survived World War II with his wife Eva in a so-called "*Judenhaus*" ("Jews' house") in Dresden, and whose diaries have made him one of the most important chroniclers of Nazi Germany, had already foreseen in late April 1919 – in his report on "leftist" street fighters – the consequences of these political developments and radicalization in a way that was clear-sighted, if not downright prophetic, in light of the calamity to come: "While they may not yet have committed murder and not yet burned Munich to ashes, they have certainly not refrained from doing everything else that must inevitably wean the unrestrained mass from a sense of justice and gradually, ultimately, lead to the worst crimes. Arbitrary arrests, hostage-taking, house searches that degenerate into the basest looting, and always, always, incitement of the worst, bloodiest, most heinous kind against the now defenseless, completely disenfranchised, completely browbeaten populace."

During the Third Reich, Klemperer viewed himself as a "cultural historiographer of the catastrophe." He met the continual demand that he placed on himself – to "observe, note, study" – by keeping meticulous notes on the everyday experience of Jewish persecution. In this Diary of a Revolution, we learn how the young Klemperer first took on this duty and, in doing so, realized that politics took precedence over everything else: "It never allowed itself to be forgotten, it infiltrated and dominated everything." This was the birth of the chronicler.

It was his uncertain academic career that originally brought Klemperer to Munich. Contrary to his expectations, he was offered a professorship at Dresden Technical College in 1920, where he taught as a salaried professor until 1935, when he was forced into retirement by the Nazis. In 1942 he wrote: "And if the Third Reich had taken nothing more from me than the opportunity to hold lectures, it would have impoverished me enough." In 1945, after the collapse of the regime of terror, Victor Klemperer was reinstated, and he remained active in academia for the rest of his life.

Chronology

Victor Klemperer

1881 Victor Klemperer is born on October 9 in Landsberg on the Warthe (today Gorzów Wielkopolski in Poland), the ninth child of the rabbi Dr. Wilhelm Klemperer and his wife Henriette (née Frankel)

1885 The family moves to Bromberg (today Bydgoszcz in Poland)

1891 The family relocates to Berlin, Albrechtstrasse 20. Klemperer's father is appointed second preacher of the Berlin Reform Congregation

1893 Klemperer attends the *Französisches Gymnasium* (French secondary school) in Berlin

1896 Klemperer transfers to the Friedrichs-Werdersche secondary school

The family moves to Winterfeldtstrasse 26[I]

1897 Commercial apprenticeship with the Löwenstein & Hecht fancy goods and notions exporter, Alexandrinenstrasse 2

The family moves to Gossowstrasse on Nollendorfplatz

1900–1902 Attends the Royal Secondary School in Landsberg on the Warthe; matriculation exam

1902–1905 Studies German and Romance philology under Franz Muncker, Erich Schmidt, Richard M. Meyer, and Adolf Tobler in Munich, Geneva, Paris, and Berlin. Prepares a dissertation under Tobler

1903 Converts to Protestantism under pressure from his family. Klemperer is baptized so that he can become a reserve officer

1905   Study visit to Rome

1905–1912   Interrupts studies and lives as a freelance journalist and writer in Berlin

1906   Marries the pianist Eva Schlemmer
Apartment on Dennewitzstrasse
Summer home in Oranienburg
Moves to Berlin-Wilmersdorf, Weimarische Strasse 6a
Glück. Eine Erzählung (Happiness: A Tale)
Schwesterchen. Ein Bilderbuch (Little Sister: A Picture Book)
Talmud-Sprüche. Eine Kulturskizze (Talmudic Sayings: A Cultural Sketch)

1907   *Paul Heyse*, a monograph
Adolph Wilbrandt, a study of his works

1909   *Paul Lindau*, a monograph
Moves to Oranienburg

1910   *Aus härteren und weicheren Tagen, Geschichten und Phantasien* (From Harder and Softer Days: Stories and Fantasies)
Berliner Gelehrtenköpfe (Berlin Academics)
Deutsche Zeitdichtung von den Freiheitskriegen bis zur Reichsgründung. Teil 1: Literaturgeschichtlicher Überblick, Teil 2: Gedichtsammlung (German Contemporary Poetry from the Wars of Freedom to the Foundation of the Reich. Part I: Literary History Overview, Part 2: Collection of Poems)

1911   Moves to Berlin-Wilmersdorf, Holsteinische Strasse

1912   Klemperer is baptized again
Moves to Munich, Römerstrasse
Resumes studies

1913   Earns a doctorate under Franz Muncker and Hermann Paul with a dissertation on *Die Zeitromane Friedrich Spielhagens und ihre Wurzeln* (The Contemporary Novels of Friedrich Spielhagen and Their Roots)
Second stay in France: produces studies of Montesquieu for a thesis to habilitate in Paris and Bordeaux

1914 Habilitates (in Romance philology) under Karl Vossler with a dissertation on Montesquieu

1914–5 Teaches at the University of Naples
Publishes *Montesquieu*, two volumes

1915 Takes oath of office as a lecturer at the University of Munich
Serves as a war volunteer (November 1915 to March 1916 on the Western front)

1916 Hospitalized in Paderborn
Awarded Royal Bavarian Military Cross of Merit 3rd Class with Swords

1916–18 Works as a censor in the book examination office of the press department of the military government in Kovno (now Kaunas, in Lithuania) and Leipzig

1918 Returns home to Leipzig in November, Reichelstrasse 16

1919 Moves to Munich, Pension Michel, Bayerstrasse 57
Moves into the Pension Berg, Schellingstrasse 1^I
Associate professor at the University of Munich

1919–20 Works as the Munich correspondent for the *Leipziger Neueste Nachrichten* under the pseudonym "A.B." (= "Antibavaricus")

1920 Moves to Dresden, Pension Blancke, Bendemannstrasse 3

1920–35 Full professor at Dresden Technical College

1920 Moves to Holbeinstrasse 131^{III}

1921 *Einführung in das Mittelfranzösische. Texte und Erläuterungen für die Zeit vom 13. bis zum 17. Jahrhundert* (Introduction to Middle French: Texts and Annotations from the 13th to 17th Centuries)
Idealistische Neuphilologie (Idealist New Philology), Festschrift for Karl Vossler on September 6, 1922, edited by Victor Klemperer and Eugen Lerch

1923 *Die moderne französische Prosa 1870–1920. Studie und erläuterte Texte* (Modern French Prose: Studies and Annotated Texts)

1924 *Die romanischen Literaturen von der Renaissance bis zur Französischen Revolution (Handbuch der Literaturwissenschaft).* (Romance Literature from the Renaissance to the French

Revolution [Handbook of Literary Studies]). By Victor
Klemperer, Helmut Hatzfeld, Fritz Neubert (by Klemperer: 1.
Introduction, 2. Italy)

1925   *Die moderne französische Literatur und die deutsche Schule. Drei
Vorträge* (Modern French Literature and the German School:
Three Lectures)
Idealistische Philologie. Jahrbuch für Philologie. (Idealist
Philology: Yearbook for Philology). Jointly edited with Eugen
Lerch. Three issues: 1925, 1927, 1927–8

1925–31   *Geschichte der französischen Literatur in 5 Bänden* (History
of French Literature in Five Volumes), Volume 5: French
Literature from Napoleon to the Present, Parts 1–3. 1.
Romanticism. 1925. 2. Positivism. 1926. 3. The Balance (The
Present). 1st Half: Bergson. The Preserved Form. 1931. 2nd
Half: The Dissolution of Boundaries. The Balance. 1931. (New
edition in 1956: *Geschichte der französischen Literatur im 19.
und 20. Jahrhundert* – History of French Literature in the 19th
and 20th Centuries)

1926   *Romanische Sonderart. Geistesgeschichtliche Studien* (Romance
Particularity: Studies in Intellectual History)
Stücke und Studien zur modernen französischen Prosa (Pieces and
Studies on Modern French Prose)
Study trip to Spain, March 13–June 14

1928   Moves to Hohe Strasse 8[I]
Romanische Literaturen (Romance Literatures). In: *Reallexikon
der deutschen Literaturgeschichte* (Lexicon of German Literary
History), Volume 3, edited by Paul Merker and Wolfgang
Stammler

1929   *Idealistische Literaturgeschichte. Grundsätzliche und anwen-
dende Studien* (Idealist Literary History: Basic and Applied
Studies)
*Die moderne französische Lyrik von 1870 bis zur Gegenwart.
Studie und erläuterte Texte* (Modern French Lyric Poetry from
1870 to the Present: Study and Annotated Texts)

1933 *Pierre Corneille*

1934 Moves into the house in Dölzschen, Am Kirschberg 19

1935 Forced to retire under the "Law for the Restoration of the Professional Civil Service"

1940 Forced out of the house in Dölzschen

Forced to move into the "Judenhaus" at Caspar-David-Friedrich-Strasse 15b

1942 Forced to move to the "Judenhaus" in Dresden-Blasewitz, Lothringer Weg 2

1943 Forced labor for the companies Willy Schlüter, Wormser Strasse 30c; Adolf Bauer, cardboard factory, Neue Gasse; and Thiemig & Möbius, paper processing, Jagdweg 10

Forced to move again into the "Judenhaus" at Zeughausstrasse 1^{III}

1945 *February*: Escapes to Piskowitz after Dresden is bombed

March 4–6: Flees via Pirna to Falkenstein in the Vogtland region

April 3: Continues to flee via Schweitenkirchen (April 6) and Munich (April 8) to Unterbernbach (April 12)

May 17: Returns via Munich (May 22), Regensburg (May 30) and Falkenstein (June 5) to Dresden (June 10)

August 19: Leaves the Protestant church

November 1: Reinstated as a full professor at Dresden Technical College (until 1947)

November 23: Joins the Communist Party of Germany

December 1: Director of the Dresden Adult Education Institute

1946 Joins the State Administration of the Cultural Association of Saxony

1947 *LTI. Notizbuch eines Philologen* (published in English as *The Language of the Third Reich*, translated by Martin Brady)

1947–60 Member of the Presidential Council of the Cultural Association for the Democratic Renewal of Germany

1947–8 Full professor at the University of Greifswald. Lives at Pommerndamm 8

1948   *Kultur. Erwägungen nach dem Zusammenbruch des Nazismus* (Culture: Considerations After the Collapse of Nazism)
       Die moderne französische Prosa (Modern French Prose), third revised edition

1948–60   Full professor at the University of Halle. Lives at Kiefernweg 10 (until 1950)

1948–50   Chairman of the State Administration of the Cultural Association of Saxony-Anhalt
       Member of the Central Board of the Society for German–Soviet Friendship

1950   Returns to Dölzschen, Am Kirschberg 19
       Delegate to the People's Chamber for the parliamentary group of the Cultural Association for the Democratic Renewal of Germany

1951   Eva Klemperer dies on July 8
       Honorary Doctor of Education at Dresden Technical College

1951–3   Member of the Central Board of the Association of Persecutees of the Nazi Regime (VVN)

1951–5   Full professor at Humboldt University Berlin

1952   Marries Hadwig Kirchner
       Receives National Prize of the German Democratic Republic, Third Class

1953   Member of the Committee of Antifascist Resistance Fighters
       Member of the German Academy of Sciences in Berlin
       Zur gegenwärtigen Sprachsituation in Deutschland (The Current Linguistic Situation in Germany), lecture
       Der alte und der neue Humanismus (The Old and the New Humanism), lecture

1954   *Geschichte der französischen Literatur im 18. Jahrhundert. Band 1: Das Jahrhundert Voltaires* (History of French Literature in the 18th Century. Volume I: The Century of Voltaire)

1956   Trip to Italy (International Congress of Romance Philology in Florence, April 3–8), study trip to Paris (April 17–July 17) *vor 33 | nach 45. Gesammelte Aufsätze* (before 33 | after 45: Collected Essays)

Patriotic Order of Merit in silver

1957 *Moderne französische Lyrik (Dekadenz – Symbolismus – Neuromantik). Studien und kommentierte Texte. Neuausgabe mit einem Anhang: Vom Surrealismus zur Résistance* (Modern French Lyric Poetry [Decadence – Symbolism – Neo-Romanticism]. Studies and annotated texts. New edition with appendix: From Surrealism to Résistance)

Trip to Paris (European Meeting on the German Question, December 14–20)

1959 Klemperer falls seriously ill in Brussels (March 28) while traveling to the International Congress of Romance Philology in Lisbon

1960 Victor Klemperer dies on February 11 in Dresden

F.C. Weiskopf Prize of the Academy of Arts in Berlin

1966 *Geschichte der französischen Literatur im 18. Jahrhundert. Band 2: Das Jahrhundert Rousseaus* (History of French Literature in the 18th Century. Volume 2: The Century of Rousseau)

1989 *Curriculum vitae. Erinnerungen eines Philologen 1881–1918* (Curriculum Vitae: Memoirs of a Philologist, 1881–1918)

1995 *Ich will Zeugnis ablegen bis zum letzten. Tagebücher 1933–1945* (published in English as *The Diaries of Victor Klemperer 1933–1945*, translated by Martin Chalmers)

Geschwister Scholl Prize of the city of Munich

1996 *Und so ist alles schwankend. Tagebücher Juni bis Dezember 1945* (And So Everything is in the Balance: Diaries June to December 1945)

Leben sammeln, nicht fragen wozu und warum. Tagebücher 1918–1932 (Collecting Life, Not Asking To What End or Why: Diaries 1918–1932)

1999 *So sitze ich denn zwischen allen Stühlen. Tagebücher 1945–1959* (So I Am Caught Between All Stools: Diaries 1945–1959)

About this edition

This first edition follows the manuscripts and printed newspaper articles held in the State Library of Saxony – Saxon State and University Library Dresden (SLUB).

The "Revolution" text is based on the handwritten original from 1942 as well as the typed copy from Hadwig Klemperer, which was created in the course of producing *Curriculum vitae. Erinnerungen 1881–1918* (2 volumes, Rütten & Loening, Berlin, 1989).

The text of the newspaper reports from the *Leipziger Neueste Nachrichten* has been taken from the newspapers published on February 11, 1919 ("Politics and the Bohemian World"), February 12, 1919 (evening edition; "Two Munich Ceremonies"), February 24, 1919 (evening edition; "Munich After Eisner's Assassination"), April 11, 1919 ("The Events at the University of Munich"), and April 10, 1919 (evening edition; "The Third Revolution in Bavaria").

The text that Victor Klemperer referred to as his "Revolutionary Diary" (including "Munich Tragicomedy") is based on his handwritten original from 1919–20. It comprises additional articles written for the *Leipziger Neueste Nachrichten* that Klemperer assumed would not reach the newspaper in time.

All texts from 1919 have been reproduced in full. To avoid unnecessary repetitions, the text from 1942 was abridged in certain places (identified by [. . .] and an explanation of the abridgement in the notes), where Klemperer had taken passages straight from the reports of

1919. The reports and memoirs have been interleaved, but no changes have been made to the sequence of the texts themselves.

The orthography and punctuation of the German texts followed the old German spelling rules (as in *Curriculum vitae*), and obvious errors and incorrect or variable spellings have been silently corrected. Text that was underlined or emphasized in another way has been printed in italics.

Picture credits

Notes

Notes in square brackets are supplied by the translator.

1 Reference to the anti-Semitic attacks leveled against Kurt Eisner in right-leaning bourgeois newspapers.

2 Kurt Eisner (1867–1919), journalist and politician; editor of *Vorwärts*, the newspaper of the Social Democratic Party, from 1898 to 1905. He joined the Independent Social Democratic Party of Germany (USPD) in 1917 and played a leading role in bringing down the Bavarian monarchy. Eisner served as chairman of the Workers' and Soldiers' Council and was elected prime minister of Bavaria on November 8, 1918. He proposed a "realpolitik of idealism" and tried to combine the councils system with parliamentarianism.

3 Reference to the elections to the constituent Bavarian State Parliament, which were held on January 12, 1919; see also note 13.

4 Erich Mühsam (1878–1934), writer and politician; member of the Central Council of the Bavarian Council Republic in 1919. He was arrested after the defeat of the republic and sentenced to fifteen years in prison, ultimately serving nearly six years of his sentence. Mühsam was arrested by the Nazis in 1933 and murdered in the Oranienburg concentration camp in July 1934.

5 The west side of Berlin was a sought-after address for journalists, writers and artists.

6 Max Levien (1885–1937), co-founder of the Communist Party of Germany (KPD) in Munich in 1919 and editor of the Munich edition of *Die Rote Fahne* (The Red Flag). As a member of the Executive Council from April 13, 1919, he was one of the leaders of the Bavarian

Council Republic along with Eugen Leviné. He was arrested in Vienna on October 7, 1919, but was not extradited to Germany. From June 1921 he lived in the Soviet Union, where he worked as an editor and lecturer in Moscow, among other activities. He was arrested again during the Stalinist purges in December 1936 and sentenced to five years in a prison camp in March 1937. On June 16, 1937, his punishment was changed to a death sentence and carried out immediately.

7 Max Levien was one of many leaders of the Left who were arrested on January 10, 1919; protesters forced their release the following day. Levien was arrested and briefly held again on February 7, 1919.

8 At the end of 1918, revolutionary workers and soldiers joined forces to form workers' and soldiers' councils which functioned as revolutionary governing bodies, replacing the old governments at the local, regional, and national levels.

9 *Leiber*: popular name for the members of the Bavarian Infantry Lifeguards Regiment.

10 Friedrich Ebert (1871–1925), Social Democratic politician, chairman of the Social Democratic Party of Germany (SPD) from 1913 (together with Hugo Haase until 1915), chairman of the SPD parliamentary group from 1916 to 1918 (together with Philipp Scheidemann). During World War I he was a proponent of the *Burgfrieden* policy (a truce between domestic political parties to support the war effort) and of a negotiated peace settlement. On November 10, 1918, he assumed joint chairmanship of the Council of People's Deputies with Hugo Haase and, with the support of the army, fought all attempts to establish a councils system in Germany. He served as Reich president from 1919 until his death.

11 Philipp Scheidemann (1865–1939), Social Democratic politician who followed the moderate line of the majority of his party during World War I. He was appointed a minister without portfolio in the government under Prince Max von Baden in 1918. On November 9, 1918, he proclaimed the German Republic and became a member of the Council of People's Deputies. From February to June 1919 he served as chancellor, heading the Weimar Coalition made up of the SPD, the Center Party, and the German Democratic Party (DDP).

12 Gustav Noske (1868–1946), Social Democratic politician, responsible for military affairs as a member of the Council of People's Deputies

(December 1918–February 1919). The January uprising of the Spartacists in Berlin was suppressed under his leadership. Noske served as Reich Minister of Defense from February 1919 to March 1920.

13 Reference to the new constituent Bavarian State Parliament elected on January 12, 1919. The Bavarian People's Party won 66 of the total of 180 seats, the SPD 61, the DDP 25, the Bavarian Peasants' League 16, the National Liberal Party 9 and the USPD 3.

14 In the fall of 1918, Klemperer was working as a non-commissioned officer in the book censorship office of the Ober Ost administrative district in Wilna (today Vilnius). In the turmoil of the revolution, he managed to obtain a travel order to Munich on Saturday, November 16, 1918, on the basis of a belatedly received request from the Bavarian Ministry of War from early November 1918; he boarded a train to Berlin at 11 p.m. that same day.

15 Klemperer's mother and the families of his six siblings lived in Berlin.

16 Eva Klemperer, née Schlemmer (1882–1951), pianist; married Victor Klemperer in 1906. She had started training as an organist in Leipzig, where Victor Klemperer had worked in the German National Library in the service of the book censorship office of the Ober Ost administrative district from mid-1916 to the fall of 1918.

17 Klemperer had voluntarily enlisted with the 7th Field Artillery Regiment "Prince Regent Luitpold" in Munich in July 1915.

18 From 1916, Victor and Eva Klemperer were members of a social circle in Leipzig which revolved around Paul Harms, a journalist and columnist for the *Leipziger Neueste Nachrichten* newspaper.

19 Klemperer had habilitated (qualified as a university lecturer) under the Romance philologist Karl Vossler in October 1914 and was sworn in as a lecturer at the University of Munich in June 1915.

20 In July 1918, apparently upon Vossler's emphatic recommendation, Klemperer had been offered a professorship at the Flemish University of Ghent ("Professorship for the Duration of the War"), but the Bavarian Ministry of War refused to release him from military duty.

21 *L'Astrée*, the most important pastoral novel in French literature (1607–27), by Honoré d'Urfé (1567–1625). Klemperer had been working on a monograph on *L'Astrée* for quite some time, but he never got further than studying the material and taking notes.

22 Philipp August Becker (1862–1947), Romance philologist; professor in Budapest in 1893, Vienna in 1905, Leipzig in 1917. He was given emeritus status in 1930 and moved to Freiburg im Breisgau as an honorary professor in the same year.

23 Hanns Heiss (1877–1935), Romance philologist; university lecturer in Bonn in 1909, professor at Dresden Technical College from 1914 to 1919 and in Freiburg im Breisgau from 1919. He was Klemperer's predecessor as the Chair of Romance Philology at Dresden Technical College.

24 Paul Harms (1866–1945), journalist, commentator and writer; earned a doctorate in Marburg in 1891 and then worked as a journalist. He was editor in chief of the *Nationalzeitung* from 1907 to 1908 and a columnist for the *Leipziger Neueste Nachrichten* from 1916.

25 Fritz Kopke (?–1933), journalist, editor of the *Leipziger Neueste Nachrichten*, and a member of the circle around Paul Harms.

26 Johannes (Hans) Scherner (1880–1947), pharmacist. He and his wife Gertrud (Trude) had met the Klemperers in May 1918 while Victor Klemperer was working in the Leipzig branch of the book censorship office of the Ober Ost administrative district (1916–18).

27 Hans Scherner had a passion for philosophy; he was attending night school to prepare for an adult *Abitur* exam that would allow him to enroll for a doctorate in the subject.

28 Eva Klemperer had started training as an organist in Leipzig toward the end of World War I.

29 Wilhelm II (1859–1941), German Emperor and King of Prussia from 1888 to 1918. When the revolution broke out on November 9, 1918, he went into exile in the Netherlands, where he abdicated on November 18, 1918.

30 The mustache style invented by the imperial barber François Haby (1861–1938), often referred to ironically as the "It is achieved" mustache.

31 The National Congress of Councils (December 16–21, 1918) decided by a majority vote to set January 19, 1919, as the date for the election of a constituent National Assembly. By choosing this very early election date (against the will of the Independent Social Democratic Party), it opted against continuing the councils system and chose the path of parliamentary democracy instead.

32 This declaration was written in January 1942.

33 Franz Adam Beyerlein (1871–1949), author of novels and plays taking a critical view of the military, including the novel *Jena oder Sedan?* (1903). He was Klemperer's successor in the Leipzig book censorship office of the Ober Ost district from July 1918.

34 *Kulturkunde* ("cultural science"), an approach followed by Klemperer after World War I, which saw in language and literature the timeless essential characteristics of different peoples, in the sense of *Völkerpsychologie* (ethnopsychology). This line of thinking was opposed by the proponents of "pure" (i.e., apolitical) literary studies, and it was tainted by the nationalist attitudes found in such works as *Esprit und Geist: Versuch einer Wesenskunde des Deutschen und des Franzosen* (*Esprit* and *Geist*: An Essay on the Nature of the German and the Frenchman) by Eduard Wechssler (1927).

35 On February 21, 1919, as he was on his way to the opening of the newly elected State Parliament where he intended to announce his resignation in light of the spectacular defeat of the USPD in the elections, Kurt Eisner was assassinated by Anton Graf von Arco auf Valley (1897–1945).

36 Bavarian slang for an infantryman.

37 "If you have boots, you can have them shined / And if you have them shined, you are a signore"; last lines of the poem "Zwei Bübchen sah ich heut" ("I saw two boys today") from the sonnet cycle *Bilder aus Neapel* by Paul Heyse (1830–1914), novelist, short-story author, poet and dramatist; awarded the Nobel Prize for Literature in 1910.

38 Berthold Kellermann (1853–1926), pianist, music teacher, and music historian; student of Franz Liszt, assistant to Richard Wagner in Bayreuth; professor at the Munich Academy of Music from 1882 to 1919. The satirical novel *Der Kraft-Mayr* (1897) by Baron Ernst Ludwig von Wolzogen (1855–1934), founder of the *Überbrettl* literary cabaret in Berlin, lampooned the popular infatuation with Wagner and Liszt before the turn of the century; the main character was modeled on Berthold Kellermann.

39 A removal company in Munich.

40 *underleinen* (Middle High German): to bolster, support; used here in the sense of "underlaid." Reference to a poem by Walther von der Vogelweide (c.1170–c.1230), "Wâz hat diu welt ze gebenne" ("What does the world

have to give"), line 9: "*dâ ist ganzer trôst mit fröiden underleinet*" ("Then the fullest confidence is bolstered with delight").

41 In a letter dated November 5, 1918, which did not reach the press office in Wilna (where Klemperer was posted) until November 16, the Bavarian Ministry of War definitively refused to discharge Klemperer so that he could take up a teaching position at the Flemish University of Ghent. It instead ordered him to return to his original unit, the Prince Regent Luitpold Regiment of the 7th Bavarian Field Artillery.

42 In July 1915, the Alphons School in Munich served as the recruitment depot for the Prince Regent Luitpold Regiment of the 7th Bavarian Field Artillery.

43 Battery emplacement in Flanders where Klemperer served from November 1915 to March 1916.

44 After an argument with Sergeant Ruhl, Klemperer had been transferred from the forward observation post back to the battery, where the hard duty led to an acute kidney infection in early April 1916, for which Klemperer was admitted to a military hospital.

45 PRL: Prince Regent Luitpold.

46 Karl Vossler (1872–1949), Romance philologist; earned a doctorate in Heidelberg in 1897, habilitated in 1899; associate professor in Heidelberg in 1902, full professor in Würzburg in 1909; worked in Munich from 1911. In 1937 he was removed from office for political reasons; after 1945 he temporarily served as rector of Ludwig-Maximilian University in Munich. Klemperer studied under him in Munich prior to World War I and habilitated under him in October 1914; Vossler encouraged Klemperer to explore the interplay between literary and linguistic history and general cultural history.

47 Franz Muncker (1855–1926), German philologist; appointed university lecturer in 1879, served as a German literary history professor from 1890 at the University of Munich. He was one of Klemperer's academic teachers; Klemperer earned his doctorate under Muncker in 1913 with a dissertation on "The Precursors of Friedrich Spielhagen."

48 *Gentes minores* (Latin): minor families, used here in the sense of less important people.

49 An associate professor; in the academic hierarchy of the time, this was a non-salaried professor whose income came solely from student fees.

50 Full professor; salaried holder of an academic chair.

51 On October 15, 1914, Klemperer had held a test lecture (on "Italian Elements in French Vocabulary at the Time of the Renaissance") at the University of Munich in order to qualify as a university lecturer; the lecture was published in the *Germanisch-Romanische Monatsschrift*, Vol. 6, 1914, pp. 664–77.

52 Eugen Lerch (1888–1952), Romance philologist; earned a doctorate in 1911, habilitated in 1914 under Karl Vossler in Munich; worked as a university lecturer, then as an associate professor at the University of Munich in 1920, as a full professor in Münster from 1930. He was forced into retirement in 1935, reinstated in Münster in 1946, and worked as a professor in Mainz from the end of 1946.

53 Erich Berneker (1874–1937), Slavist; professor in Breslau in 1909, appointed to the newly established Chair of Slavic Philology in Munich in 1911.

54 Clemens Baeumker (1853–1924), philosopher; professor in Breslau in 1883, then in Bonn and Strasbourg, worked in Munich from 1912.

55 In German, *meritorisch*: meritorious; on the merits.

56 Gustav Kafka (1883–1953), philosopher; professor of philosophy and education at Dresden Technical College in 1923, forced to retire in 1934, reinstated at Dresden Technical College in 1946, worked in Würzburg from 1947.

57 Leo Jordan (1874–1940), Romance philologist; associate professor at the University of Munich in 1911, lecturer for Romance languages at the Munich School of Business 1913–23; honorary professor at the Technical University of Munich in 1923. He was dismissed on July 21, 1933, on account of his Jewish heritage, and he committed suicide in July 1940.

58 Fritz Strich (1882–1963), Swiss literary scholar; associate professor in Munich from 1915, full professor in Bern from 1929 to 1953.

59 Hans Heinrich Borcherdt (1887–1964), German philologist; university lecturer in 1915, professor in Munich from 1920, later director of the Institute for Theater History in Solln near Munich.

60 Christian Janentzky (1886–1968), German philologist; professor of German language and literature at Dresden Technical College 1922–52, director of the university library from 1945 to 1948.

61 Otto Crusius (1857–1918), Classical philologist, professor in Munich from 1903.

62 Klemperer means Magda (Magdalena) Muncker, the wife of Franz Muncker.

63 *Potator* (Latin): drinker.

64 Eugen Lerch's first wife, Sonja (née Rabinowitz), born 1882 in Warsaw. She earned a doctorate in Giessen in 1913 with a dissertation on the development of the Russian labor movement; in January 1918 she was arrested with Kurt Eisner in Munich as the "ringleader" of a munitions workers' strike and charged with treason; at the same time, she and her husband divorced; in April 1918 she committed suicide while in custody.

65 At the time, Eugen Lerch was working on a study of "The Use of the Romance Future Tense as an Expression of Moral Obligation"; it was awarded the Samson Foundation Prize of the Bavarian Academy of Sciences and Humanities and was published in 1919 in Leipzig.

66 Reference to Adolf Tobler (1835–1910), Swiss Romance philologist, professor in Berlin from 1867. He spent decades collecting material for an "Old French Dictionary" that was published starting in 1915 by Erhard Lommatzsch et al.

67 In 1914–15 the expanded version of Klemperer's doctoral dissertation, a two-volume monograph on the philosopher and political theorist Charles-Louis de Secondat, Baron de La Brède et de Montesquieu (1689–1755), was published by the Winter publishing house of Heidelberg University as part of its series *Beiträge zur Neueren Literaturgeschichte – Neue Folge* (Contributions to Modern Literary History – New Series).

68 While lecturing at the University of Naples in 1914–15, Klemperer had hoped to be appointed to the Royal Academy of Posen (today Poznań).

69 In volume two of Klemperer's autobiography *Curriculum Vitae*, in part four ("The Ghent affair and the end of the war") of chapter three ("Soldier"), Klemperer recounts a discussion in July 1918 with Philipp August Becker, a Romance philologist in Leipzig, in which Becker refers to Klemperer's appointment in Ghent as a "great stroke of luck." When Klemperer asks why, Becker explains "with exhaustive detail": "Because you will only get a professorship by coming in from the outside, never in the usual way. You're Vossler's disciple, and Vossler is notorious for being

eccentric, unprofessorial. You were a journalist for eight years before pursuing an academic career, and you became a lecturer far too quickly and easily [. . .]. Your Montesquieu is much more of a literary work than a strictly philological one – do you think you'll be forgiven for all that? But you'll manage it with this foreign professorship [. . .]" (pp. 635f.). In connection with this, Klemperer wonders whether his academic career to date could be compared to a ride across Lake Constance, with the Ghent professorship lying on the opposite shore. [In German, a "ride across Lake Constance" (*Ritt über den Bodensee*) is a risky undertaking, the dangers of which are only apparent after the fact; based on a nineteenth-century ballad by Gustav Schwab, "Der Reiter und der Bodensee."]

70 The internists Georg (1865–1946) and Felix Klemperer (1866–1932) and the lawyer Berthold Klemperer (1871–1931) provided regular financial support to their brother Victor until he was appointed as a professor at Dresden Technical College.

71 Hans Meyerhof (1881–1951), Klemperer's friend since they had been apprentices together at the Löwenstein & Hecht export company in Berlin in 1897–9; Meyerhof was living in Munich with his companion, Elena Marwerth, at the time of Klemperer's visit.

72 See previous note.

73 *Simplicissimus* was a weekly political satire magazine founded in Munich in 1896; it was fiercely critical of German society, especially prior to 1914.

74 Bruno Frank (1887–1945), novelist and short-story writer, also a playwright and poet; emigrated in 1933 via Austria, Switzerland, France, and England to the USA.

75 Bruno Frank's play *Die Schwestern und der Fremde* (The Sisters and the Stranger) premiered in Munich in 1918.

76 Arthur Schnitzler (1862–1931), Austrian playwright and author.

77 Bruno Frank's essay was published in 1919 in Munich under the title of "*Von der Menschenliebe*" ("On Altruism").

78 *Centenaire de Voltaire*, speech for the centenary of Voltaire's death, delivered by Victor Hugo in 1878.

79 Stanislaus Stückgold (1880–1939), Polish painter and graphic artist; studied at the Warsaw Academy of Fine Arts in 1905–6, then lived abroad; leaned heavily toward symbolism.

80 Cf. the sarcastic and ironic characterization of the evening by Thomas Mann in his diary entry from December 10, 1918, in: Thomas Mann, *Tagebücher 1918–1921*, pp. 105f. (edited by Peter de Mendelssohn, S. Fischer, Frankfurt, 1979).

81 Reference to the Independent Social Democratic Party of Germany (USPD), which had spun off from the Social Democratic Party (SPD) in 1917 out of opposition to the *Burgfrieden* policy of the party leadership; it supported the councils system from 1919. The party's right wing reunited with the SPD in 1922 after the left wing had aligned itself with the Communist Party of Germany in 1921.

82 Karl Liebknecht (1871–1919), politician; in December 1914 and August 1915 he was the only Social Democrat in the Reichstag to vote against the approval of war loans. He was a co-founder of the Spartacus League and the Communist Party of Germany and played a leading role in the left-wing socialist uprising against the Majority Socialist government of Ebert and Scheidemann in January 1919. On January 15, 1919, Liebknecht was arrested with Rosa Luxemburg and murdered by Freikorps soldiers.

83 Hotel Trefler on Sonnenstrasse in Munich.

84 Hans Unterleitner (1890–1971), Bavarian Social Democratic politician, Kurt Eisner's son-in-law; Minister for Social Welfare from November 1918 to April 1919, member of the Reichstag (first for the USPD, later for the SPD) from 1920 to 1933, imprisoned in Dachau concentration camp from 1933 to 1935, escaped to Switzerland in 1936, emigrated to the USA in 1939.

85 *Oxytone* (Greek): word with the stress on the last syllable.

86 *Schmock*: a hack, an unprincipled journalist; named after a character in Gustav Freytag's play "The Journalists" (1854); the word frequently had an anti-Semitic undertone.

87 The reporter Wippchen was the most successful character created by the humorous writer Julius Stettenheim (1831–1916); "Wippchens sämtliche Berichte" ("The Full Reports of Wippchen") were published in sixteen volumes from 1878 to 1903.

88 A recurring character in the satirical magazine *Ulk* (1872–1934), founded by Rudolf Mosse and Siegmund Haber; the character was created by Hermann Scherenberg (1826–97), a painter, graphic artist, illustrator, and caricaturist.

89 Andreas Latzko (1876–1943), Hungarian author who wrote in German; formerly an officer, emigrated to England in 1938; *Men in War*, his volume of pacifist novellas, was published in 1917.

90 Henri Barbusse (1873–1935), French novelist, poet and journalist; his antiwar book *Le feu* (1916, published in German as *Das Feuer* in 1918) made him famous.

91 Karl Escherich (1871–1951), forestry scientist and entomologist; professor at the Tharandt Academy of Forestry from 1907 and at the University of Munich from 1914 to 1936; it was not him, as Klemperer assumed, but rather his older brother, the forestry official Georg Escherich (1870–1941), who founded the Organization Escherich ("Orgesch") in mid-1921 after citizens' militias had been banned in Bavaria. Orgesch grew to one million members in Bavaria and Austria and was responsible for numerous right-wing-extremist attacks and assassinations.

92 Georg Heim (1865–1938), Bavarian politician known as the "peasant doctor"; organizer of the agricultural cooperative system in Bavaria, co-founder of the Bavarian People's Party (BVP) in 1918.

93 Reference to the party color of the Catholic-oriented German Center Party.

94 Ludwig III (1845–1921), Prince Regent in 1912, King of Bavaria from 1913 to 1918.

95 Reference to Ludwig II (1845–86), King of Bavaria from 1864.

96 Klemperer worked as a lecturer at the University of Naples in 1914–15.

97 Fritz Neubert (1886–1970), Romance philologist; earned a doctorate in Munich in 1910, habilitated in Leipzig under Philipp August Becker in 1918 and then worked as a lecturer; appointed associate professor in Leipzig in 1923, worked as a full professor in Breslau in 1926 and in Berlin in 1943; confirmed as a professor in Berlin in 1946; worked at the Free University of Berlin from 1949 to 1956.

98 Annemarie Köhler (1892–1948); studied medicine and then worked first as a surgeon in the Johanniter (Order of St. John) hospital in Heidenau near Dresden and later in her own private clinic in Pirna with Dr. Friedrich Dressel. She became a close friend of Victor and Eva Klemperer in the mid-1920s; from 1940 she kept Klemperer's manuscripts and diaries for him so they would not fall into the hands of the Gestapo if Klemperer's house were searched.

99 The Carl Köhler factory was founded in 1854 in Crimmitschau (Saxony) and produced pure wool textiles for men's clothing; Annemarie Köhler's father, Emil Köhler, was a co-owner of the company.

100 Ella Doehring, secondary school teacher, acquainted with Victor Klemperer since his second study trip to Ghent in 1904; she died in August 1920.

101 Reference to the surgeon Friedrich Dressel (1892–1991).

102 Franklin Punga (1879–1962), electrical engineer; professor of electrical engineering at Darmstadt University of Technology from 1921; head of the Institute for Electrical Machines there from 1921 to 1949.

103 A secondary-school leaving certificate was also known as a one-year (*Einjährige*) because young men with this educational qualification had to perform only one year of voluntary military service instead of the usual three years. These men were called one-year volunteers, and the secondary-school leaving certificate was considered an "academic qualification for one-year voluntary military service."

104 Rosa Luxemburg (1870–1919), leading theorist in the left wing of the SPD; imprisoned as a radical opponent of the war from March 1915 until November 1918 (with a brief hiatus); drafted the program for the newly founded Communist Party of Germany (KPD) at the end of 1918; was arrested and murdered by Freikorps soldiers on January 15, 1919, together with Karl Liebknecht.

105 *Leipziger Neueste Nachrichten*, founded in 1892 under the leadership of Edgar Herfurth as the successor to the *Leipziger Nachrichten*; the paper followed a nationalist-conservative line and quickly developed into one of the most important and widely circulated daily newspapers in Germany.

106 *Ruth*, a novel (Cotta, Stuttgart, 1895) by Lou Andreas-Salomé (1861–1937), novelist, essayist and psychoanalyst.

107 Reference to the German Democratic Party (DDP), founded on November 20, 1918, as a successor to the Progressive People's Party and parts of the National Liberal Party. The party program was influenced by Friedrich Naumann's ideas about socially responsible liberalism. In the National Assembly elections on January 19, 1919, the DDP took 18.5% of the votes and 75 mandates, making it the third-strongest party after the SPD and the Center Party.

108 In German: *über dem Strich* (above the line). In the newspapers of the time, the space *unter dem Strich* (under the line) at the bottom of the page was reserved for arts and culture, while political articles were published above this dividing line.

109 Edgar Herfurth (1865–1950), founded the Edgar Herfurth & Co. publishing house in 1892 together with his brother Paul Herfurth (1855–1937); the newly founded company took over the *Leipziger Nachrichten* which, under the new name of *Leipziger Neueste Nachrichten*, quickly became one of the leading and most widely circulated daily newspapers in Germany.

110 The elections to the Prussian constitutional convention were held on January 26, 1919; the Majority Socialists won with 36.4% of the votes, coming in ahead of the Center Party (22.3%), the German Democratic Party (16.2%) and the German National People's Party (11.2%); the USPD received 7.4% of the votes.

111 From April 17 to early May 1919, Klemperer took the reports he had written for the *Leipziger Neueste Nachrichten* about the events in Munich and consolidated them in a "Munich Revolutionary Diary." It partially took the place of the diary he continued to keep. The "Revolutionary Diary" has remained unpublished until now.

112 "Curriculum," Klemperer's shorthand for his *Curriculum vitae*, the autobiography he wrote between February 1939 and February 1942.

113 In July 1934, Klemperer first mentioned in his diary that he intended to write a study of "the language of the Third Reich." The first time he used the abbreviation "LTI" to refer to this work was in his diary entry from July 8, 1941: "lovely scholarly abbreviation for *lingua tertii imperii* [(Lat.) Language of the Third Reich], to be used henceforth." – Immediately after the end of the war, in the summer of 1945, Klemperer began using his diary entries to explore the connection between the ideology and language of National Socialism. His study was published in German in 1947 under the title of *LTI: Notizbuch eines Philologen* (LTI: A Philologist's Notebook) by Aufbau-Verlag in Berlin, and it made an important contribution to illustrating the ideological mechanisms of the Nazi regime. (The English translation, *The Language of the Third Reich*, translated by Martin Brady, was first published in 2000 by The Athlone Press.)

114 Ferdinand Lotheissen, *Geschichte der französischen Literatur im XVII. Jahrhundert* (History of French Literature in the Seventeenth Century), four books in two volumes, Vienna, 1877–84.

115 Gustave Lanson, *Histoire de la littérature française*, Paris, 1894.

116 Klemperer first mentioned his idea "for a study of the state in Corneille's dramas" in a diary entry from February 13, 1919. He wrote the essay between April 19 and 24, 1919, and it was published under the title "Vom Cid zum Polyeucte" (From Cid to Polyeucte) in the journal *Die neueren Sprachen*, Vol. 28, 1920, pp. 413–48; it also appears in Victor Klemperer, *Romanische Sonderart. Geistesgeschichtliche Studien* (Romance Particularity: Studies in Intellectual History), published by Max Hueber, Munich, 1926, pp. 52–103. Klemperer wrote his monograph on Corneille in 1931–2; it was published in early 1933 (the last of his books to be published for a long time) as Number 3.1 in the series *Epochen der französischen Literatur* (Epochs of French Literature), also by the publishing branch of the Max Hueber university bookstore.

117 French: *je suis nu* – I am naked; *je suis né* – I was born.

118 Plays by Friedrich Schiller: *Die Räuber* (1781), Schiller's first play; *Don Carlos* (published 1787); *Wallenstein* (published 1800), a trilogy of plays.

119 Leo Ritter (1890–1979), surgeon; head physician in the surgical gynecology department of the Hospital of the Order of St. John of God in Regensburg from 1929 to 1964.

120 Ferdinand Sauerbruch (1875–1951), surgeon; professor in Marburg in 1908, Zurich in 1911, Munich in 1918, from 1925 in Berlin.

121 Michael von Faulhaber (1869–1952), professor in Strasbourg in 1903, Bishop of Speyer in 1911, Archbishop of Munich-Freising in 1917, cardinal in 1921; resolutely opposed the racism of Hitler's regime after 1933.

122 In the spring of 1916, Klemperer was in a Catholic hospital in Paderborn with an acute kidney infection.

123 *Winterreise* (1828), song cycle by Franz Schubert for voice and piano.

124 Arnold Weißberger, later Weissberger (1898–1984), photochemist from Chemnitz; earned a doctorate in 1924 and habilitated in 1928 in Leipzig; emigrated to England in 1933 and then to the USA in 1936, where he worked for Eastman Kodak Co. in Rochester, New York.

125 Eduard Weißberger (1868–1935), chemist; authorized signatory for Bachmann & Ladewig AG, Chemnitz.

126 Arnold Weissberger had already habilitated, or qualified as a lecturer, in 1928.

127 Freikorps regiment under the command of Major General Wolf, founded in Augsburg, existed from April to August 1919 and was made up of more than 600 men.

128 Reference to a possible professorship at Dresden Technical College, where the Romance Philology chair had become vacant after Hanns Heiss was appointed to Freiburg in 1919.

129 The first of several reports Klemperer wrote about the events in Munich in the first half of 1919 for the *Leipziger Neueste Nachrichten*; this dispatch was published in issue number 40 on February 11, 1919, under the headline "Politics and the Bohemian World," and it was signed "From our A.B. correspondent." The abbreviation "A.B." that Klemperer used as a pseudonym stands for "Antibavaricus."

130 Regarding the distribution of seats, see note 13.

131 Independent Social Democratic Party (USPD).

132 Franz Mehring (1846–1919), journalist and politician; originally a bourgeois democrat, but started moving closer to the SPD in 1891; editor in chief of the Social Democratic *Leipziger Volkszeitung* from 1902 to 1907, teacher at the central SPD party school from 1906 to 1911; co-editor of the *Sozialdemokratische Korrespondenz* in 1913–14; co-founder of the Spartacus League in 1916, moved to the USPD in 1917, participated in the foundation of the Communist Party of Germany (KPD) at the end of 1918. Franz Mehring had died in Berlin on January 28, 1919.

133 Gustav Landauer (1870–1919), writer and politician, representative of a romantic-anarchistic form of socialism. He was encouraged by Kurt Eisner on November 14, 1918, to participate in the revolution in Bavaria. He drafted the text proclaiming the Munich Council Republic together with Erich Mühsam and served as Commissioner for Public Enlightenment in the first council government. Landauer was arrested on May 1, 1919, when the Council Republic was defeated. He was murdered one day later by Freikorps soldiers while being transferred to the Stadelheim prison in Munich.

134 Georg von Hertling (1843–1919), politician for the Center Party; Reich

Chancellor from November 1, 1917, to September 30, 1918; died in Ruhpolding on January 4, 1919.

135 Reference to the LZ-4 dirigible, which crashed and burned near Echterdingen on August 4, 1908, during what was intended to be a 24-hour test flight from Friedrichshafen to Basel, Strasbourg, Mainz and back again to demonstrate the military capability of airship technology. The catastrophe triggered a wide-scale aid campaign in Germany that enabled Count Ferdinand von Zeppelin (1838–1917) to continue his work.

136 Eduard Weckerle (1890–1956), journalist; member of the USPD, later of the Socialist Workers Party (SAP), then the SPD from 1932; emigrated to Switzerland in 1933.

137 Else Eisner (née Belli, 1883–1940), editor; Kurt Eisner had begun living with her around 1910. They were married in 1917 after Eisner divorced his first wife, Elisabeth (née Hendrich), with whom he had two sons and three daughters, and from whom he had separated in 1905 after thirteen years of marriage. Kurt Eisner had two daughters with Else Eisner. Else Eisner emigrated to France after 1933. In June 1940, as German troops were advancing, she took her own life.

138 Reference to the student Anton Graf von Arco auf Valley (1897–1945), reserve lieutenant (member of a student corps or fraternity); he assassinated Kurt Eisner on February 21, 1919.

139 The Theresienwiese is a very large open space in Munich.

140 Erhard Auer (1874–1945), Social Democratic politician; member of the Bavarian State Parliament from 1907 to 1933, member of the Reichstag as well from 1919; Bavarian Minister of the Interior under Kurt Eisner from November 1918.

141 Reference to Kurt Eisner's appearance at the Bern International Socialist Conference of February 1919.

142 Felix Fechenbach (1884–1933); Kurt Eisner appointed him as a secretary in the state chancellery in November 1918; in 1922 he was sentenced to eleven years in prison by the Munich People's Court for supposed high treason in the so-called "German Dreyfus Affair" initiated by the journalist Paul Nikolaus Cossmann; the sentence was overturned by the Supreme Court of the German Reich in 1926. While working for the *Volksblatt*, an SPD newspaper, from 1929 to 1933 in Detmold, he

wrote many well-informed articles about the affairs of Nazi Party leaders. He was arrested in March 1933 and murdered on a transport to the Dachau concentration camp on August 7, 1933.

143 Erhard Auer was severely wounded in an assassination attempt carried out by USPD supporter Alois Lindner immediately after Kurt Eisner was murdered on February 21, 1919; Auer stepped down as Bavarian Minister of the Interior but continued to lead the Social Democrats in Bavaria until 1933.

144 Bavarian army barracks built in 1823 in the Maxvorstadt district of Munich (on the Türkengraben canal).

145 The Lotter Putsch on February 19, 1919, was a failed attempt to overthrow Kurt Eisner initiated by Konrad Lotter, a sailor and member of the Bavarian Soldiers' Council.

146 On February 21, 1919, representatives of the SPD, USPD, and KPD, as well as all executive bodies of the workers', peasants' and soldiers' councils and the Revolutionary Workers' Council, formed a Central Council of the Bavarian Republic. This "eleven-man committee" functioned as a provisional governmental body until April 7, 1919. During this time, the debate about a "council government or parliamentarianism" grew more fierce. On March 4, 1919, a council congress rejected the formation of a coalition consisting of the SPD, USPD, and Bavarian Peasants' League, but on March 17 the State Parliament elected Johannes Hoffmann as prime minister.

147 Reference to Klemperer's article entitled "Munich After Eisner's Assassination (from our A.B. correspondent)" in: *Leipziger Neueste Nachrichten*, evening edition from February 24, 1919, no. 53, p. 3.

148 Anton Graf von Arco auf Valley (1897 to 1945), reserve lieutenant; he assassinated Kurt Eisner on February 21, 1919.

149 Alexander Strasser, member (probably chairman) of the Revolutionary University Council of the University of Munich; after the defeat of the Council Republic, he and his fellow student Otto Hausdorf were sentenced to one and a half years in prison "with a probationary period."

150 Johann Wolfgang Goethe, *Aus meinem Leben: Dichtung und Wahrheit* (From My Life: Poetry and Truth), 1811–2.

151 Josef Schick (1859–1944), Anglicist; professor in Heidelberg from 1893,

in Munich from 1896 to 1925. Klemperer had attended the University of Munich in the summer semester of 1902.

152 Mary Schick (née Butcher); Josef Schick had met her in Devon during the three years he spent in England (1884–7).

153 Paul Joachimsen (1867–1930), historian, secondary-school teacher, honorary professor at the University of Munich from 1916, and his wife Margarethe.

154 Carl (or Karl) Hamecher; later ran a specialist philately store at Luisenstrasse 4 in Munich; co-founder of the Association of Bavarian Stamp Dealers together with Curt Mohrmann.

155 *Bon sens* (French): common sense.

156 Short for *Rezensions-Exemplar*, or review copy.

157 Survey of French Syntax.

158 On April 7, 1919, the Bavarian Council Republic was proclaimed by the Central Council of the Bavarian Republic under Ernst Niekisch and by the Munich Central Workers' Council.

159 Johannes Hoffmann (1867–1930), Social Democratic politician; Majority Socialist, culture minister in the Bavarian government formed in November 1918; appointed prime minister on March 17, 1919, by the newly elected State Parliament; formed a minority cabinet comprising representatives of the SPD, USPD, and Peasants' League. After the Council Republic was proclaimed on April 7, 1919, he and his government fled to Bamberg. During the Kapp Putsch in March 1920, he was forced to resign by the Reichswehr.

160 Friedrich Alfred Schmid Noerr (1877–1969), German philologist, philosopher, writer; university lecturer from 1906, associate professor of philosophy in Heidelberg from 1910 and in Munich from 1917 to 1918; drafted a plan of action for "Revolutionizing the Universities" on behalf of Gustav Landauer and the Revolutionary University Council of the University of Munich in April 1919, then worked as a freelance author. He was close to the conservative wing of the resistance against the Nazi regime (he composed a Draft of the Constitution of the German Reich in 1937–8 on behalf of Ludwig Beck).

161 "Memorandum for drafting a new university constitution. On behalf of the 'Society for New Education,'" developed and drafted by Friedrich Alfred Schmid Noerr, Steinicke, Munich 1919.

162 Max Weber (1864–1920), sociologist, economist and economic historian; held teaching posts in Berlin, Freiburg im Breisgau, Heidelberg, and Vienna, was a professor in Munich from 1919. Weber was instrumental in establishing sociology as an independent academic discipline.

163 Klemperer is referring to the imminent end of the semester and start of the semester break.

164 Schwabing was known as the bohemian quarter of Munich.

165 Reference to the brothers Gregor and Otto Strasser. Gregor Strasser (1892–1934), member of the Nazi Party from 1921, participated in the Beer Hall Putsch in Munich in 1923, was appointed Reich propaganda leader in 1926. At the end of 1932, contrary to Hitler's wishes, he spoke out in favor of the Nazi Party's participation in a right-wing coalition; in the subsequent dispute he was stripped of all Party offices. He was murdered on June 30, 1934, during the Night of the Long Knives. Otto Strasser (1897–1974) was a member of the SPD from 1917 to 1920, then joined the Nazi Party in 1925; as head of the Kampfverlag publishing house in Berlin and a representative of the left-leaning faction of the Nazi Party, he came into conflict with the Party leadership. After openly breaking with Hitler, he founded the Black Front in 1930 and continued agitating against Hitler after 1933 from abroad; he lived in exile until 1955. No evidence has been found that Alexander Strasser was related to the brothers Gregor and Otto Strasser.

166 Friedrich von Müller (1858–1941), internist; held teaching posts in Bonn, Breslau, Marburg, and Basel from 1889, was a professor in Munich from 1902.

167 Klemperer actually took his oath of office as a lecturer at the University of Munich on June 7, 1915.

168 Ludwig Quidde (1858–1941), historian and politician; opponent of the policies of Wilhelm II; associated with the German Peace Society from 1894 (chairman 1914–29), member of the German Democratic Party (DDP) after 1918. Quidde received the Nobel Peace Prize in 1927 (together with Ferdinand Édouard Buisson). He emigrated to Switzerland in 1933.

169 Franz Lipp, lawyer (earned doctorate in Heidelberg in 1880); served as People's Commissioner of the Exterior under Ernst Niekisch from April 7, 1919, but only held office for a few days on account of mental illness.

170 Ernst Toller (1893–1939), dramatist, poet and novelist; during the Munich Council Republic in April 1919 he served as chairman of the Bavarian Workers' and Soldiers' Council and commander-in-chief of the Dachau Front; he wrote the majority of his works during the five years he subsequently spent in prison. Toller was forced to emigrate in 1933 (via Switzerland, France, and England to the USA); on May 22, 1939, he committed suicide in New York.

171 Otto Neurath (1882–1945), Austrian economist; lecturer under Max Weber in Heidelberg; after April 7, 1919, while serving as president of the Central Economic Planning Office of the Bavarian Council Republic, he began to introduce a moneyless economy; after the defeat of the Council Republic he was sentenced to 18 months in prison, but the sentence was not enforced on account of protests from Austria. Neurath subsequently worked in Vienna until he was forced to flee to The Hague in 1934; he was able to emigrate to England in 1940.

172 Arnold Wadler (1882–1951), social scientist (earned a doctorate in Munich in 1907); was appointed Minister of Housing in 1918 under Kurt Eisner; on April 8, 1919, while acting as the commissioner for housing, he ordered all residential property in Bavaria to be "seized and rationed"; he emigrated to Switzerland in 1933, and later to France; in 1940 he was able to escape to the USA.

173 Franz Ritter von Epp (1868–1946), regiment commander in World War I, then a Freikorps leader; left the Reichswehr as a major general in 1923 and joined the top leadership of the SA; became a member of the Reichstag for the Nazi Party in 1928, then Reich Governor in Bavaria in 1933, and was interned by the American occupying authorities in 1945.

174 Franz Epp was appointed major and commander of the 2nd Battalion of the Lifeguards Regiment in 1912, then promoted to lieutenant colonel and commander of the Lifeguards Regiment at the end of 1914; he was knighted in 1916.

175 Line from the first stanza of Franz Grillparzer's poem "Field-marshal Radetzky" written in June 1848: "Lead on, Commander, lead our cause! / 'Tis more than glory beckons, / Austria is united in your camp / While we are scattered fragments." Franz Grillparzer: "Field-marshal Radetzky", translated by Robert Russell, in: *Discourses of Collective Identity in Central and Southeast Europe (1770–1945), Volume II:*

National Romanticism – The Formation of National Movements, edited by Balázs Trencsényi and Michael Kopeček, Budapest/New York: Central European University Press, 2007, pp. 436–9.

176 On Monday, April 7, 1919, the Bavarian Council Republic was proclaimed under the leadership of Ernst Niekisch (1889–1967), one of the three USPD representatives in the newly elected Bavarian State Parliament. In 1920, Niekisch was sentenced to two years in prison for his involvement in the Council Republic. He later became a leading proponent of the National Bolshevist ideology that influenced the Strasserist wing of the Nazi Party. After 1933 he was a leader of the conservative resistance against Hitler. He was arrested in 1937 and sentenced to life imprisonment for high treason in 1939.

177 *Un silence tragique* (French): a tragic silence; dramatic quiet.

178 Ernst Schneppenhorst (1881–1945), trade unionist and SPD politician; Minister for Military Affairs in the cabinet of Bavarian Prime Minister Johannes Hoffmann from March–August 1919; member of the Reichstag 1932–3; active in the resistance from 1933; arrested in 1944 and murdered by the Gestapo in Berlin in April 1945.

179 Emil Aschenbrenner, one of the commanders of the Republican Protection Force stationed at the central train station, which was loyal to Hoffmann's government in Bamberg. On April 13, 1919, Aschenbrenner led the Palm Sunday Putsch against the Council Republic, during which some members of the Central Council (including Erich Mühsam) were temporarily detained.

180 Olaf Gulbransson (1873–1958), Norwegian painter and illustrator; leading staff member of the satirical magazine *Simplicissimus* in Munich from 1902.

181 Rudolf Egelhofer (1896–1919), participant in the Kiel sailors' mutiny; after the Palm Sunday Putsch was defeated, he was appointed city commandant of Munich and commander-in-chief of the Red Army. He was shot by members of the Freikorps as they marched into Munich.

182 *Nutrimentum spiritus* (Latin): food for the soul.

183 Described in Victor Klemperer's report "Two Munich Ceremonies. By A.B." in: *Leipziger Neueste Nachrichten*, evening edition from February 12, 1919, no. 41, p. 3.

184 On April 16, 1919, three days after KPD functionaries led by Eugen

Leviné and Max Levien seized power in the Council Republic, Landauer announced his resignation from all political roles and offices in the Council Republic.

185 After the Council Republic was overthrown, Gustav Landauer was arrested on May 1, 1919. One day later, as he was being transferred to the Stadelheim prison in Munich, he was murdered by Freikorps soldiers.

186 This is followed by a passage that Klemperer took from his A.B. dispatch of April 19, which is printed in the following, in which he summarizes the events from "Finally the tribunal appears" (p. 90) to "threatening to fire in the dark hallway" (p. 92).

187 *Briefe aus der Französischen Revolution* (Letters from the French Revolution), selected, translated, and annotated by Gustav Landauer, Rütten & Loening, Frankfurt am Main, 1919 (two volumes).

188 Reference to characters in the play-within-a-play performed by the mechanicals in William Shakespeare's *A Midsummer Night's Dream*.

189 Reference to Eduard Weckerle.

190 *Reservatrechte*, special sovereign rights granted by Bismarck to both Württemberg and Bavaria when the German Empire was unified in 1871; the rights applied to, among other things, the military, the postal service, and telegraphy.

191 Lydia (née Rabinowitz – married name unknown) was the sister of Sonja Lerch (née Rabinowitz), who had committed suicide in April 1918. Lydia Rabinowitz was divorced and had a son who was around ten years old at the time.

192 Emil K. Maenner, People's Deputy for Finance in the Munich Council Republic.

193 Hans Meyerhof.

194 Paul von Lettow-Vorbeck (1870–1964), general; commander of the so-called "protection force" in German East Africa from 1914 to 1918, accepted into the Reichswehr in 1919, dismissed for participating in the Kapp Putsch in 1920.

195 In a short section here, Klemperer took excerpts directly from his A.B. reports from April 30 and May 2, 1919, starting with the "prominent rumble of trains" (p. 103), through "But immediately afterwards the *Rote Fahne* called for all-out resistance" (p. 105), "The 'unarmed' was

heavily emphasized" and "everyone said the Ostbahnhof had been taken by Prussians in the night" (p. 110), to "That was the start of the 'counter-revolution' here" (p. 111).

196 This is where Klemperer included the depiction of the Potsdam death's-head hussars (pp. 112).

197 *Horribile dictu* (Latin): terrible to say.

198 Albert Döderlein (1860–1941), gynecologist; professor in Tübingen in 1897, appointed to Friedrich von Winckel's chair in Munich in 1907, which he held until his retirement in 1934. Döderlein was not among the murdered hostages.

199 On April 30, 1919, soldiers from the Red Guard, whose commander, the sailor Rudolf Egelhofer, had held supreme authority in Munich since April 29th, shot ten previously imprisoned hostages, including eight members of the nationalist and anti-Semitic Thule Society, in an attempt to deter the government and Freikorps troops that were advancing on the city.

200 Arnold Ritter von Möhl (1867–1944), Bavarian major-general; while serving as commander-in-chief of the Bavarian Army Command which was formed in early 1919 (though he was actually under the supreme command of the Prussian General Ernst von Oven), he defeated the council regime in Munich and established a military dictatorship that ruled by means of martial law until August 1919. On March 14, 1920, during the Kapp Putsch, he was appointed Bavarian State Commissioner at the urging of the Reichswehr. He was removed from internal Bavarian politics when he was appointed commander-in-chief of Reichswehr Group Command 2 in Kassel in 1923, and he was dismissed from the Reichswehr with the rank of *General der Infanterie* in 1924.

201 Ernst von Oven (1859–1945), Prussian *General der Infanterie*; actual supreme commander of the Bavarian Army Command, which was formed in early 1919 in coordination with the Reich government and commanded by Bavarian Major-General Arnold Ritter von Möhl, and which led the operation to crush the Bavarian Council Republic. The troops of the Bavarian Army Command took control of Munich on May 3, 1919, and more than 600 people were killed in the city in the following week. After the fighting ended, the Bavarian Army Command exercised military authority in Bavaria, but by May 11, 1919, it had already been integrated into the Reichswehr as Group Command 4. From 1922, Ernst

von Oven was commander-in-chief of Reichswehr Group Command 1. Burghard von Oven (1861–1935), who retired as a *General der Infanterie* in 1920, is sometimes erroneously said to have been the head of the Reichswehr operation against the Bavarian Council Republic.

202 Cf. note 143.

203 From the start of the fighting to the defeat of the Council Republic, 606 casualties were reported, 38 of whom were members of the government forces and Freikorps; another 400 people were subsequently shot and killed, including 52 Russian prisoners of war who were executed by Freikorps members in a gravel pit near Gräfelfing.

204 On May 6, 1919, government soldiers shot 21 members of a Catholic journeymen's association in their clubhouse; they had been falsely denounced as Spartacists.

205 When this section of the "Revolutionary Diary" appeared in the *Leipziger Neueste Nachrichten* (published as a feature article under the headline "Munich After the Liberation" on pages 1 and 2 of the evening edition from May 14, 1919; no. 120), this was erroneously printed as "*Hausrecht*" (householder's rights) instead of "*Standrecht*" (martial law). In Klemperer's diary entry from May 18, 1919, he writes: "The 'Schill' article [. . .] was published by the L.N.N. as a feature on Wednesday evening 14/5. But characteristically, the subordinate clause was lost from the sentence: 'Then the troops went into a frenzy as well and exercised martial law, *even when a court martial would not have imposed a death sentence.*' Regardless, my article is still nonpartisan enough. A few nasty misprints, such as 'phrenetic,' *Hausrecht* instead of *Standrecht*. After the fate of my revolutionary diary, I was so delighted with the publication that first I mercilessly read the thing to Eva, who had returned dead tired from many hours in the academy, then to Hans M., whom I visited before supper, then Heilbronn and Reyersbach, with whom we sat in Café Stephanie and who then came up to our rooms."

206 Ernst Toller was sentenced to five years in prison, all of which he was forced to serve.

207 Ferdinand von Schill (1776–1809), Prussian officer; he took it upon himself to attack French troops with his regiment in 1809 in an attempt to force the Prussian king to act; he was killed during the defense of Stralsund.

208 Otto Hausdorf, member of the "Revolutionary University Council"; after the defeat of the Munich Council Republic, he was sentenced to a year and a half in prison "with a probationary period."

209 Well-known saying based on a comment by Prussian administrative lawyer Traugott von Jagow (1865–1941), who served as chief of police in Berlin from 1909 to 1916, in an announcement relating to a left-wing demonstration: *"Die Straße gehört dem Verkehr. Ich warne Neugierige"* ("The street is for traffic. A warning to the curious!").

210 Franz von Epp joined the Nazi Party on May 1, 1928, and played a leading role in the Nazis' seizure of power in Bavaria. He was appointed Reich Commissioner of Bavaria on March 9, 1933, at which point he transferred police power to *Gauleiter* Adolf Wagner and named Heinrich Himmler as chief of police in Munich. On April 10, 1933, three days after the announcement of the Second Law for Coordinating the States with the Reich, he became Reich Governor of Bavaria.

211 Matthias Meier (1880–1949), philosopher; student of Clemens Baeumker, university lecturer from 1914, associate professor in Munich from 1920, professor in Dillingen from 1923, professor at Darmstadt University of Technology from 1927.

212 The Weimar Coalition, made up of the SPD, the Catholic Center Party, and the left-liberal German Democratic Party, held 330 of 423 seats in the constituent National Assembly; it formed the government of the Reich in 1919–20 and 1921 and the government of Prussia in 1919–21 and 1925–32.

213 Hans Meyerhof visited Victor and Eva Klemperer in Dresden in February 1921 on a trip through Germany; they next saw each other eight years later, in March 1929, when Victor and Eva Klemperer met him and Elena Marwerth at their home in Palermo while traveling by ship from Genoa via Sicily to Hamburg.

214 Quote from the play *The Prince of Homburg* by Heinrich von Kleist, Act II, Scene 10.

215 Walther von Dyck (1856–1934), mathematician; professor at the Munich Polytechnic (later the Technical University of Munich) from 1884, its rector from 1919 to 1920; played a leading role in establishing the Deutsches Museum in Munich.

Index